MW01089388

STOICISM FOR MODERN TIMES

3 BOOKS IN 1 - A BLUEPRINT TO BUILD INNER PEACE, RELIEVE STRESS, CONQUER YOUR FEARS, OVERCOME ADVERSITY & LEAD A GOOD LIFE

CONTENTS

STOICISM FOR STRESS RELIEF

A Blueprint To Stop Worrying, Calm Your Mind, Relieve Stress, and Find Inner Peace with Stoics

THE POWER OF STOICISM
24 Stoic lessons to live happier, care less, master your emotions & become unshakable like a Stoic

THE POWER OF STOICISM

9 Laws from Stoics to Build an
Unbreakable Mind, Forge Resilience,
Conquer Your Fears, and Become
Unshakable in Face of Adversity

STOICISM FOR STRESS RELIEF

A BLUEPRINT TO STOP WORRYING, CALM YOUR MIND, RELIEVE STRESS, AND FIND INNER PEACE WITH STOICS

ALSO BY ALEXANDER CLARKE

Visit my author page

author.to/alexanderclarke

YOUR FREE GUIDE

To help you control your mind I've created a guide with 9 easy tools from Stoics to build mental strength. Make sure you download it at the following URL:

alexander-clarke.com

It will help you greatly on your personal development journey. The stronger you train your mind to be, the more you will control your thoughts.

If you want to master your mind and your emotions make sure to grab this free guide!

PREFACE

Do something for me. Sit back, relax, and try to count the number of times you've heard people say the word "stress" and the number of people you've seen visibly stressed. Are you making any headway with that? The chances are, they are too many.

Who would have thought that stress would become one of the most popular words in our society?

Admittedly, stress has a profound effect on our lives. No wonder more people are talking about stress in the world today, and no wonder stress levels have risen in the last several years. Thankfully, with this expanding discussion has come more information about stress, its sources, and its impact.

You may have perceived stress to be a mere feeling of being overwhelmed, but it's much more than that. Stress comes in many forms, each with its own physical and psychological side effects. Let's talk about what it means to be stressed.

WHAT DOES IT MEAN TO BE STRESSED?

We experience stress when we see an event or situation as a danger or challenge. Hence, stress is defined as a sensation of emotional pressure and strain when we are unable to manage situations or are feeling overwhelmed.

A flurry of chemicals and hormones is released throughout our bodies when we are under stress. Many of us are already acquainted with the fight-or-flight reaction that this causes. What you might not know is it also impacts our metabolism, memory, and immune system, to name a few.

TYPES OF STRESS

There are four common types of stress - acute stress, episodic acute stress, chronic stress, and burnout. Let's take a look at each of them.

1. Acute Stress

Your body's response to a new or demanding environment is what causes acute stress. Some unusual circumstances or unexpected events that may cause acute stress include; divorce, speaking engagements, exams, interviews, and so many more. The symptoms of this kind of stress only present for a short time and leave after the stressful event has passed. It turns out that acute stress is sometimes good for our bodies. It helps us overcome ourselves and adapt to dangerous circumstances. It's a short-term type of stress. In most cases, our emotions and body recover very fast.

2. Episodic Acute Stress

If you experience frequent acute stress, that is known as episodic acute stress. It could be as a result of work deadlines, stressful relationships, high expectations of yourself, and so forth. Healthcare personnel, for example, are subjected to stressful conditions on a regular basis. This kind of stress is episodic acute stress. We don't have time to return to a peaceful and relaxed condition while we're under this kind of pressure. Furthermore, the negative consequences of this frequent, high-intensity stress build up over time and leave us feeling like we're always in the middle of a new crisis.

3. Chronic stress

Chronic stress is the outcome of long-term stressors, like having a stressful job or having frequent fights with your spouse. Left unchecked, this stress that lasts for an extended period may have a severe impact on your health. You experience chronic stress when the body's autonomic nervous system is unable to trigger the relaxation response on a regular basis because of the frequency or severity of the stressors. To put it another way, the body is always in a state of physiological alertness. Practically every organ and system in your body feels the effects of this alertness. This is why stress that lasts for a long time is not compatible with the way humans were designed to live. It negatively impacts many elements of your health and well-being, sometimes without your realization.

4. **Burnout**

Everyone experiences burnout at some point in their lives. Working, volunteering, or caring for our families may keep us quite busy in our day-to-day lives, and this is perfectly normal. However, burnout occurs when we fail to rest as needed. It is a state of tiredness brought about by a persistent sense of being overburdened. It's a consequence of long-term emotional, physical, and mental strain. Workplace stress is a common cause of burnout.

We suffer from burnout when we feel overwhelmed, emotionally exhausted, and unable to keep up with life's constant demands. Although it is not a medical condition, if you don't recognize or manage burnout, it may have a negative impact on your physical and emotional health. It may negatively impact your personal, professional, and social life. Some major causes of burnout are; workloads that are too much to handle, workplace discrimination, workplace obligations that are difficult to discern, managers' lack of communication or support, and so many others.

WHERE DOES STOICISM COME IN?

People have developed many coping mechanisms to deal with stress. The adaptiveness and usefulness of these tactics vary, as do their efficacy. Stoicism does better in managing stress than any coping mechanism would, because it is a life philosophy.

A coping mechanism means you're still dealing with the problem and have merely found a way to live with it. But with stoicism, stress doesn't even have to be a problem. What I am about to introduce you to is a lifestyle. My goal is to help you permanently win the fight against stress by giving you one of the most effective weapons. With this philosophy, you're not just letting go of stress for good, you are going to develop a whole new outlook on life that will help you live a purposeful and full life. Welcome to the school of stoicism!

INTRODUCTION

"The happiness of your life depends on the quality of your thoughts."
— **Marcus Aurelius, Debts and Lessons**.

Welcome to the stoic life, where there is no stress and absolutely no worries. We take you to your inner Chi and help you connect with your soul, where you find peace.

If that's what you were expecting me to say, you guessed wrong. Stoicism is not a lifehack. It is a method of living and, to put all cards on the table, if you're going to live a Stoic life, you'll have to work hard. There are no two ways about it. This is not a unique thing about stoicism. It is true of all real-life philosophies. Prepare to give it your all as you dive right in. My aim is not for you to simply learn about stoicism but to understand and use it as a means to relieve stress and attain inner peace.

I want you to implement real stoicism in your life by working with the practical advice I give in this book and adapting it to your modern-day life and struggles. I know that reading about stoicism is often difficult because most books are either too academic, complex, or just too much for beginners. So, I have created this book with deep roots in traditional stoicism yet adapted for the modern man. Yes, I am committed to helping you make this work.

The question then becomes, what is stoicism? As simple as it seems, this is one question that is very difficult to answer. One of the major things that has made it difficult to answer is the many wrong perceptions of stoicism in the world today. For instance, the Oxford English Dictionary defines "stoicism" as a state of mind in which one suppresses their emotions and maintains their composure in the face of hardship. That couldn't be further from the truth.

Over the last few centuries, we have been exposed to depictions of ancient Stoic philosophy by classical writers like Cicero, Seneca, and Plutarch. However, as with many popular stoic ideas, we find that, while their ideas may have some truth, they are far from comprehensive. To get a good understanding of what stoicism truly is, we have to backtrack a little. We have to go back to 300 BC when Zeno the Citium established stoicism. The "Stoics" got their name from an informal gathering at Athens' Painted Stoa, a covered colonnade on the northern side of the Agora (markets). Plato's Academy and Aristotle's Lyceum were still thriving, but Zeno's contemporary, Epicurus, was establishing his own school just outside the city gates.

The Cynics, a group of philosophers who were influenced by Socrates' example, also thrived in this period. The Stoics had no official school property and were gathering at a public site in the center of the city. Cleanthes, a student of Zeno's, continued attracting a big audience after Zeno's death. Chrysippus, regarded as the most significant early Stoic after Cleanthes, replaced him as his successor. This tradition of teaching at the Painted Stoa may have lasted until the first-century BC. Rome had risen to become the dominant cultural and political power in antiquity by this point. In the Romanized world, Stoicism prospered because the Romans found many of its principles appealing.

In the first century BC, Cicero availed many major explanations of Stoic philosophy to Latin speakers. From Diogenes of Babylon in the East, Seneca of southern Spain, Emperor Marcus Aurelius, the Near-Eastern immigrants in Athens, and to members of the Imperial court in Rome, Stoicism appealed to a broad spectrum of people. There were many Stoics in Rome during this period, including Seneca, Lucan, Persius, Musonius Rufus, and Epictetus. Emperor Marcus Aurelius' *Meditations*, written in the second century, represents the pinnacle of Roman Stoicism's absorption by the Romans.

The mass appeal of the philosophy is why, although we have only a few references to ancient stoic writings, we understand that Stoicism isn't just a set of intellectual assumptions about how we may know the world or what we should do, but rather an attitude or way of life. Stoicism is rooted in a specific idea of what philosophy is, and as a result, its philosophical theories of ontol-

ogy, epistemology, and ethics are rather complicated. The Stoics see philosophy as essentially
concerned with how one should live.

However, the Stoics were not the only ones who
believed this, as the ancient Epicureans and
Cynics did as well. In other words, how was the
Stoic way of living different from the other ancient philosophical schools' proposals? The Stoic
method of thinking is based on philosophical
ideas of ontology, epistemology, and ethics that
resemble those advanced by contemporary
philosophers. The Stoics offered a materialist ontology in which God penetrates the whole world
as a material force. According to them, one's
goodness is all that is needed to be happy, and
other factors such as wealth and circumstances
are of secondary importance. A sort of cognitive
psychotherapy, they said, may help people overcome their negative feelings. The ideal Stoic sage
was depicted as flawlessly logical, dispassionate,
indifferent to his or her surroundings, and, no-
tably, joyful even when tortured on the rack. Stoicism's intellectual significance continued even
after its popularity waned in the early third
century.

Even though nearly all the original texts of the Athenian Stoics have been lost, the school's ideas have continued to influence later philosophers. First through the widely available Latin texts of Cicero and Seneca in the Middle Ages, and then through collections of fragments from the early Stoics culled from various ancient authors who cited or reported on their writings.

Stoicism had a major impact on the development of philosophy in the sixteenth and seventeenth centuries and was one of the many forces that led to its growth. Stoic concepts were well-known to writers like Erasmus, Calvin, Montaigne, Descartes, Pascal, Malebranche, and Leibniz. Throughout this time period, Stoicism was frequently brought up in discussions about the ego, human reason, destiny, free choice, and emotions. Later works by Michel Foucault and his analysis of "self-care" as well as "technology of the self" are a clear indication of the continuing impact of Stoicism in modern times. As a result, not only was Stoicism a popular philosophical school in antiquity, but it has remained so throughout Western philosophy's history.

For a variety of reasons, dissecting Stoicism as a philosophical system is a difficult undertaking.

The majority of the earliest writings have vanished. As a result, we must depend on subsequent accounts written by people who were either antagonistic to Stoicism or writing in an intellectual context that was substantially different from today's. It is difficult to establish how faithfully they represent previous Stoic dogma and how much they include subsequent changes. Regardless of all these, from an adequate study of stoicism there is no doubt that stoicism is a method for achieving self-mastery, endurance, and wisdom, not some arcane academic subject of research.

Stoicism is a way of life that prices above all things, moral excellence. Stoics live by three basic beliefs. First, they believe that virtue is sufficient for happiness. Secondly, stoics hold that the good things in life should be regarded with indifference and finally, they believe that the world is ordered by God, in his providence. We will camp on the first two in this book. We will answer the questions: how can I pursue virtue as an immunization against stress, and what things am I letting define me that shouldn't? The goal? To help you to live a stress-free life using timeless stoic wisdom. If this sounds like what you came here hoping for, read on.

1

STRESS IS TIMELESS; WE ARE NOT

"We suffer more in our imagination than in reality."
— **Seneca, Letter From a Stoic.**

If you honestly believe that the Stoics were immune to stress, you have it all wrong. The majority of the founding fathers and proponents of stoicism faced extreme stress. There is every possibility that their being overwhelmed with stress led them to seek out the philosophy.

Consider the founding father himself, Zeno. He lost everything he owned in a shipwreck. Imagine that! His experience was certainly traumatic. Seneca also had his fair share of stress in his lifetime. For many years, he had to labor in Nero's court, constantly dodging the unpredictable antics of a man who had uncontrollable bloodlust.

As you can appreciate now, stress has been a timeless phenomenon. The ancient Stoics were stressed beyond measure because, unlike us, they had no advanced technology to help them take care of some of their problems. They did not have many plausible ways out of their stress. Like them, at some point in our lives, our responsibilities tangle and get in the way of each other. We all face some sort of pain, failure, loss, or hardship. Even the stoics knew these were all unavoidable as long as you were alive. But how were they able to conquer stress? Simple, by changing their perception of it.

FEELING STRESSED IS A CHOICE

Stress is inevitable, but is suffering because of it compulsory? No. Look at it this way, going to school is mandatory for all of us, but the way we see school determines whether it will be a time of learning for us or a walk through the fires of hell. Stress is assured, but being stressed out is not. The two don't always have to go together.

This is one of the secrets that kept the Stoics one step ahead of any other philosophy in regards to stress. Marcus Aurelius, in *Debts and Lessons*, declared that he could choose not to feel hurt in order not to feel hurt. Although this might seem unsensible at first, it's exactly what he meant. Stress is a constant in life, and there's no escaping it, but it is a conscious choice to feel and stay stressed. Ultimately, the choice to feel stressed is up to us. You don't have to be stressed. You don't have to panic, and neither do you have to live in fear.

Adopting stoicism as a way of life is a great way to combat the issue of stress in our lives. However, contrary to what many think, stoicism does not encourage us to deal with stress by running from it. The philosophy, more than any other, embraces an active life. It encourages us to participate in anything that makes our lives worth living without succumbing to the tensions accompanying many of these activities.

This kind of teaching is what Marcus Aurelius is famous for. His writings are full of personal notes on how to contain his anger and avoid the uneasiness that follows not reacting. Epictetus also embraced this perspective in life as he continually urged his students to focus on what they could control, like their studies.

Seneca was also popular for propagating this theory by constantly warning his students not to suffer before it was required. This largely resonates with the words of William Shakespeare, who tells us, "A coward dies a thousand deaths, a hero dies but once."

The discipline of perception helps us understand that there is no need to stress over what we cannot control. For instance, from ancient Stoic teachings, we learn that we control our brains but not our outer circumstances. This means that rather than focusing on outer circumstances, we can control our reactions to them. If we grasp this, then stressful situations will no longer bother us.

If you want to be able to manage what you can and ignore what you can't, here's what you can do:

1. Consider the source of your anxiety.
2. How long have you been feeling this way?
3. How much power do you have over your situation?

4. If you have some power, what can you do to modify or enhance the current situation?

If modifying the situation is not an option (for example, you have a terrible boss and you have no control over it), consider shifting your perspective on the source of your stress. To do this, look at it from various perspectives and select the one that causes you the least amount of anxiety. If you're ready to grasp this, keep reading.

WHAT ARE STRESSORS?

The first step to ending stress in your life is to identify your main stressors.

But what is a stressor? Anything around or within you that activates or triggers the production of stress hormones is a stressor. These things could be either physical or mental. Physical stressors are things like injuries, sickness, and all forms of pain that can be inflicted on our physical bodies. In comparison, mental stressors are triggers that arise from events, people, opinions, or anything that we might consider harmful to our minds. Mental stressors often come in the form of words.

It is important to note that we are not all stressed by the same things. Although most of your stress falls in any of these categories, you must identify the specific stress source in your life to deal with it.

HOW TO IDENTIFY STRESSORS?

A stressor is an occurrence or condition that creates anxiety or tension. Almost anything may be a source of stress as long as it is viewed as a threat. Keep in mind that stress is a natural reaction to danger. The best way to identify your stressors is to zoom into the major aspects of your life .

- Physical - It might be your physical surroundings, in terms of bright lights, noise in your area, discomfort due to excessive heat, discomfort due to extreme cold, weather, and traffic.
- Psychological - It could also be your psychological environment. In addition to rudeness or violence in others, disagreement with others, failing to

spend enough time with essential people, a lack of social support, and loneliness might all be contributing factors to your stress level.

- Financial - Your financial situation could also be causing you stress. Taxes, unpaid bills, unexpected costs, the strain of "making ends meet," and various other factors may be making your life hard.

However, there is good news. Adopting stoicism will remove these stresses from our lives, regardless of the source of the stressors in question. I earlier mentioned that these stressors can be physical or mental. The next section will explore them in full detail.

Possible physical stressors

To identify your stressor, you have to look for it. We are often confused about the things causing us stress, anxiety, and worry. Our inability to calm down and search is why you hear people say things like, "I am fed up with life." If you don't want to get there, you need to ask yourself questions about the major aspects of your life - your job, your home, your relationships, and your city. Which one do you think is causing you the most stress and worry? Why is it stressing you?

1. Assess your physical environment

Our physical surroundings, such as where we live and the people we interact with daily, both in our own homes and in our larger communities, make up our environment. Everything from your home, city, and state to the weather, the social atmosphere, and your workplace may have an impact on your mental health. If you spend a lot of time in these areas, they may profoundly affect your physical and mental health.

2. Assess your level of engagement

The second step in identifying your stressor is to find out if you're overwhelmed. We are often stressed by the number of engagements we sign up for. Is it possible that you have bitten off more than you can chew? We also constantly ignore the fact that idleness can cause anxiety, depression, and stress. Could it also be that you're not doing enough?

3. Check your eating habits

Our food has a big role in how we feel both mentally and physically. This is why your diet could be the source of your stress. Anxiety and depression have been closely linked to excessive consumption of fast and processed food. Several research studies have shown that you feel better when you eat better.

4. Observe your sleeping habits

Poor sleeping habits could be causing your stress. Our generation glorifies being "booked and busy," but we fail to understand that we need sleep to function properly. Lack of adequate sleep usually has a rippling effect on your quality of life. For instance, when you don't sleep well, you become more irritable throughout the day, and even things that normally should not be considered stressful become a struggle. Whenever you feel stressed, check your sleeping habits because more often than not, good sleep puts us in a good mood.

5. Check your caffeine intake

A cup of coffee in the morning has become the norm in our society, but caffeine could be to blame for your nervousness and anxiety. The Archives of General Psychiatry says that coffee may increase or even cause anxiety in those who don't ordinarily experience it. Rather than cutting out caffeine completely, Gerst suggests giving it up for a week to see whether it makes a difference.

Possible mental stressors

1. Check your relationships

Relationships are a constant source of mental and emotional stress for many people. Often, we are not aware that the people we associate with are stressing us. You must observe how your body reacts in the presence of your friends. Do you become nervous or feel intimidated when it's time to hang out with these people? Then they may be a stressor for you. You can do this with anybody - a colleague, acquaintance or even partner. Any relationship can become toxic. So, do not put boundaries on who you can assess.

2. Check your mind

A major trigger for stress can be consistently worrying over what we cannot control. We often put ourselves in mental prisons trying to "prepare for the worst," which never happens. Is it possible that your stress comes from always imagining the worst?

3. Check your self-image

A low view of yourself can be a major source of mental stress. This may be the case for you if you constantly set yourself up for failure by indulging in self-criticism and self-sabotage.

4. Check how you deal with change

Stress may accompany every big life event, including joyous ones like marriage or a job raise. A divorce, a huge financial loss, or the death of a family member may cause substantial stress. What is your view on change? Do you welcome change and adapt to it or do you fight it? Fighting change can create stress in your life and when you are stressed, other important parts of life like eating a balanced diet or working out tend to fall off the wagon causing even more stress. Examine yourself to see what you find uncomfortable about change and what your default response is. Are you resistant to all change or only specific changes in your life?

5. Check your expectations

Sadly, society - through social media - paints a picture of perfection. This usually causes us to have extremely high expectations that are bound to stress us out. If things don't go according to plan, do you get anxious?

6. Check you social media use

Social media could be another major source of stress for you. Although it has its benefits, it's easy to get lost on social media and allow ourselves to be subjected to unnecessary pressure. This can present itself as social media addiction consisting of excessive worry about likes and follows, an uncontrolled impulse to log on or use social media, and excessive time and effort devoted to social media.

When social media is used as a coping method to alleviate stress, loneliness, or despair, it becomes problematic. People who share pictures online may get positive social feedback, which causes the brain to produce dopamine, which encourages them to continue posting. It's because they're constantly being rewarded for their social media use that they wind up using it more often. Your negative emotions might get worse if you continue using the device for long periods, disregarding real-life relationships, job or school duties, and physical health.

7. Are you multitasking?

For a long time, multitasking was seen favorably, so you might be surprised to see it here. By doing two things at once, like sending emails while watching TV or texting plans for the next day while completing schoolwork, you can be considered productive, but that may not be the case.

Studies by Stanford University in 2009 titled "Cognitive Control in Media Multitaskers" reveal that focusing our attention on a single task helps us become more productive and less stressed. Multitasking might harm mental health, according to the study.

The Stanford University study on the possible damage to the brain from multitasking discovered that persons who attempt to concentrate on many streams of electronic information simultaneously have a lower capacity to do one activity properly. Memory and concentration have been shown to suffer when people multitask. According to the research, people who multitask have more difficulty remembering facts than those who focus on one activity at a time. Multitaskers had lower attention spans than individuals who just worked on one thing at a time.

8. Analyze your financial situation

Another major source of your mental stress could be your finances. Financial pressure is when you're feeling anxious or worried about your money. Financial strain may strike anybody at any time, with the volatile economic market we have in the world. Not being able to pay your rent, utility bills, and food expenses may cause stress.

Financial strain usually has a ripple effect on other things in our lives, because it often causes us to overwork. People who earn less money may be more stressed out by their work. If your work schedules don't allow you to take time off or your job is risky, that could be the source of your stress.

2

YOUR VIEW, YOUR PERCEPTION

*"Things stand outside of us, themselves by themselves,
neither knowing anything of themselves nor
expressing any judgment."*
— **Marcus Aurelius, Meditations.**

We have gone through the major stressors and seen examples of what could constitute the stressors in your life. Now we want to deal with them.

One of the best ways to deal with stress is how the stoics did, by changing your perception, as we stated earlier. But what is perception? Thanks to the dictionary, you might think of perception as how you view a thing or a particular situation. But that's not all there is to perception.

Stoic perception is more than just the way you view a particular situation; it is about a way of life. In stoicism, perception is a mindset determined by how you choose to see yourself in life. What does this mean? There are two ways to see ourselves; you could see yourself as a victim or a victor. The way you see yourself will determine how you perceive any situation you find yourself in.

Hence, perception goes beyond how we look at certain situations. It is our mindset on who we are in life. But, we don't just determine who we are in life in one sitting; it takes a lot of observing and training. This is why, in this chapter, we will be retraining our minds on how to perceive stressful situations and how we see ourselves.

PERCEPTION AND STRESS

Although the concept of perception is quite broad, we are narrowing it down to how it can help us eliminate stress in our lives. We must agree that many factors influence our perception of ourselves and our situation to do this. If that's true, it's not as easy as saying that what we see is an accurate representation of reality. The Stoics believed that reacting to the world is entirely up to you; nothing else is. They argue that most of the time, you have a choice in how you respond to any given circumstance.

However, you have to keep in mind that your re-action is shaped by your perceptions, which are shaped by your convictions. Your convictions are connected to your thoughts, and negative thoughts can take root in your mind over time if they are not dealt with. Suffice to say, our reac-tion to anything changes as our beliefs about it shift. There is good news - we can improve our lives, be more effective in our responses, and lessen the impact of stressful or painful events.

HOW TO CHANGE YOUR PERCEPTION?

1. Choose gratitude daily

One of the significant sources of stress is the lack of contentment. We push ourselves beyond breaking point trying to get the things we don't have rather than appreciating what we have. Epi-curus in Epicurea once said, "Do not spoil what you have by desiring what you have not; remember that what you now have was once among the things you only hoped for." If you want to preserve the good things in your life, keep in mind that they were once only a dream.

From Stoicism to Buddhism, the idea of cultivating an attitude of gratitude is touted as a means to a more contented and resilient existence. Changing our perspective is all it takes to alleviate the feeling that we lack something in our lives or don't have what we want.

Instead of obsessing over the things you don't have right now, it pays to be grateful for them because if you lose them you'll miss them, right? Stop glorifying the things you don't have and start seeing the value in what you take for granted. The gratitude mindset helps us disrupt the need-want-buy cycle that we have found ourselves in as a society. Just imagine you weren't chasing after anything you don't have, and you were content in just enjoying what you have right now; how relaxed would you be?

The more thankful we are, the less we want the things we don't have. We become happier and more satisfied. Start looking at life from the perspective that you have many of the things you wanted. And even if you didn't wish for them, be grateful that you have them because if you didn't, you would need them. We are happy when we have a greater appreciation for what we already have. Stop stressing yourself trying to get what you don't have. Make it a practice to express gratitude and appreciation for all of life's blessings, and you'll see how things that you considered a burden and a source of stress begin to become a privilege to you.

2. See obstacles as opportunities

Like I stated earlier, stress is a choice. You can either choose to allow something to stress you or do something about it. Many of the things we consider stressful today are situations that we would easily surmount and come out winners if we choose to see them as opportunities for learning. In the words of Marcus Aurelius in Meditations 5.20: "The impediment to action advances action. What stands in the way becomes the way." In my words, I would say, "When anything stands in the way, it becomes the way itself." Or at least, it should.

What happens to us is out of our hands, but we have complete power over how we respond to it. In the face of adversity, you may either choose to whine or seek a solution. When you choose to whine and complain, you remain in the hardship, but when you choose to seek a solution, you make a way through that hardship. This is the best way to live - making a way through hardship and turning obstacles into the way. It is the only way to live because resilience, reliability, and insurmountability can only be achieved by embracing misfortune and looking for opportunities in it. With this attitude, you will never be held back by hardship; you will lessen the pain it causes and develop strong resilience.

3. Take responsibility

You can change your perception by taking responsibility for whatever situation you find yourself in. There are always two approaches to finding yourself in unfortunate predicaments. You could blame someone or something else for your predicament, or you could come to terms with the fact that what has happened has happened; but what you do after is up to you. The way you react is up to you, even if you didn't cause everything that's occurred. You're the only one who is accountable for your thoughts and feelings. It's up to you to choose whether to be a victor or a victim.

However, when you blame someone or something else, you relinquish the responsibility for your well-being. You're letting someone or something else take the wheel of your emotions and drive you wherever they want. How stressful! Many factors cause our negative moods, but we must still take responsibility for our condition, find out what's going on, and develop a solution. Mostly, laying blame is a waste of time and exacerbates the situation. Placing blame forces you to revisit the past, and if you keep doing that, you will never come out of the rut.

4. Don't judge

In the beginning, we were all blank slates. As we got older, our brains absorbed more and more information, allowing us to recognize things like forms, colors, feelings, and different dialects or languages. Our brains were busy creating a network of connections, analogies, and patterns to organize everything. In that sense, we are formed by the people and things around us, including our family, friends, instructors, the places we visit, and the books, music, and movies we consume. As a result of our past experiences, we're the people we are now.

Sadly, not everyone is lucky enough to grow up in a positive environment, and we face hardships of varying degrees. Many people are born into poverty, violence, and lack of decent role models, and they are often left to fend for themselves.

Some of us have to deal with adversity at a young age, while others have an effortless time. Both of these scenarios have significant drawbacks, though. Understanding others' experiences might help us become more sympathetic to one another if we consider ourselves to be defined, in part, by our own experiences. When we know what other people have gone through, we can better comprehend their behavior.

5. Decide to let go of your anxiety

How do you manage the anxiety you feel about a problem or a situation? Here's how the Stoics knew how to handle their anxiety. During his life, Marcus Aurelius faced many challenges that an emperor must face - wars and pressure of power. He wrote in his journal "Today I escaped from anxiety. Or no, I discarded it, because it was within me, in my own perceptions."

What this means is that he made a conscious choice to abandon his anxiety and leave it at the door. Remember, if you can create something inside you, you can also get rid of it, by making a conscious choice.

3

YOUR ANGLE, YOUR CONTROL

"The chief task in life is simply this: to identify and separate matters so that I can say clearly to myself which are externals not under my control, and which have to do with the choices I actually control. Where, then, do I look for good and evil? Not to uncontrollable externals, but within myself to the choices that are my own...."
— **Epictetus, The Enchiridion.**

C hanging your perception will be useless if you are not concerned about the right things. It will be like doing the right thing for the wrong person. Epictetus knew this when he introduced the concept of mental rewiring. In stoic philosophy, this process is known as the dichotomy of control. It is one of the most critical and profound principles of stoicism. Fortunately, it's also one of the most straightforward concepts.

THE DICHOTOMY OF CONTROL

It is the Stoic principle of separating things under our control from those beyond our control. This is how Epictetus states it in his book, "The Enchiridion":

1. Things that are within your control: your thoughts and actions.
2. Things that are outside of your control: everything else.

It is possible to stop spending time attempting to manage things you can't and instead concentrate on those things over which you can have some degree of control. Lucky for us, there are a lot of things under our control. Some of them are; what you think, what you want, what you do, and how you respond to things. The other things we cannot control are your health, fortune, reputation, and the past, to list some.

If you're thinking, "Wait a minute, why can't I control those things?" You're not alone! Now, really think about it. Do you have any actual power over your health? Every day of the week, you could go for a run, get a good night's sleep, and follow a healthy diet. However, you might still be diagnosed with a fatal disease. That is why you have no influence over anything save your ideas and behaviors. Not even the most diligent, health-conscious person is immune to sickness. We may try to affect the results, which is a good idea, but we don't have any actual control over things like that.

There is no control over what happens, but you have power over your reaction to it. In the words of Epictetus, "There are things which are within our power, and things beyond our power. Within our power are opinion, aim, desire, aversion, and, in one phrase, whatever affairs are our own. Beyond our power are body, property, reputation, office, and whatever things are not properly our own affairs."

STRESSING IS A WASTE OF TIME

To understand the duality of control, you first need to understand why you should quit worrying in life. Let's take, for example, that you decide to get a coronavirus test since you are not feeling well. The doctor informs you that the results will be available a few days after the test. Yet as soon as you go back home, you start worrying about the test results.

You fail to sleep or eat for three days because you are so scared. Then the results come, and you're negative, so you stop stressing over it. Is there anything to show for all the stress? No. What if, however, the test results were to be positive? It's the same story. Your worrying only causes you to suffer twice, once before receiving the results and again after.

Just like Seneca said in "Letters From A Stoic," "We suffer more often in imagination than in reality." To put it another way, you shouldn't stress about anything in life at all. Do not allow something you cannot change to upset you. And when it's something you can change, rather than worry, fix it. Worrying, in any case, does nothing. As Epictetus puts it, "there is only one way to happiness, and that is to cease worrying about things which are beyond the power of our will."

DON'T WORRY TOO MUCH ABOUT WHAT OTHERS THINK

"It never ceases to amaze me: we all love ourselves more than other people but care more about their opinion than our own."
– Marcus Aurelius, Meditations 12.4

I want to address one thing we often worry about and think is in our control but is not - the opinion of others. The fact is, you have no control over what other people think of you, among a slew of other things. We've learned so far that if you can't control something, don't worry about it. Worrying about how others view you is a waste of time and energy.

Yes, it is alright to consider constructive criticism, but the highlight is on the "constructive" part. It is okay to accept the criticism of others if it is helpful. But other people's views are not supposed to be such a great source of concern that you cannot move on with your life.

There are three primary ways for you to filter criticism.

1. Ask yourself if the critic is someone you value and respect.
2. Can you trust that the person delivering criticism is sincere?
3. Do you benefit from their criticism?

UNDERSTANDING SUCCESS: THE STOIC ARCHER

There is a balance to this message of not stressing. Yes, you might not control the result of an event, but you may strive to influence it to the best of your ability. Think of it as an arrow being shot by an archer: Even with the most refined posture, the best-built bow, and the straightest arrow, the archer's success or failure is not in his hands. A blast of wind, a flying bird, or an unsecured target could all intercept the arrow mid-flight.

Regardless of how hard you try, things might go awry and prevent you from reaching a goal. However, if you didn't give it your all, you've already lost. To get the desired result, all you can do is concentrate on what you have control over. The same rules apply, whether it's a job interview, romance, or an exam. The balance is this - there is no assurance that you will succeed, no matter how hard you try. Instead of focusing on winning the game, focus on giving your best performance on the field.

TAKE A CHANCE

"It's something like going on an ocean voyage. What can I do? Pick the captain, the boat, the date, and the best time to sail. But then a storm hits. What are my options? I do the only thing I am in a position to do, drown — but fearlessly, without bawling or crying out to God, because I know that what is born must also die."
– Epictetus, The Enchiridion.

You also have complete control over whether or not you decide to do anything at all. If you don't even attempt, you're sure to miss out on the opportunity to reach your objective. The only thing you can control is whether you take the shot and give it your best effort, whether you're shooting an arrow, going for a job interview, or approaching a stranger in the bar.

Keeping in mind the duality of control will significantly assist you in taking risks. It relieves you of unneeded strain and helps you to operate in the consciousness that you have already succeeded by trying your best - success then, is in the effort, not in the result. Rather than stress over the worst happening, I say stress over the best happening, if it's any stress at all.

EVERYTHING DEPENDS ON YOUR OPINION

"If any external thing pains you, it is not this thing that disturbs you, but your judgment about it. And it is in your power to wipe out this judgment now."
– Marcus Aurelius, Meditations 8:47

Let's say even after exerting every ounce of effort, a project fails. Most people respond with anger, irritation, or depression. But what good do any of those feelings do? Some people believe that these feelings are legitimate since they are human. Yet it's also true that animals have feelings; what sets us apart from them is our ability to reason. Regardless of how you feel about it, our capacity to reason is what sets humans apart from other creatures.

Rather than relying on our feelings, we climbed to the top of the food chain by using logic. As a result, it is your responsibility to choose how you respond to every situation. Remember the dichotomy of control - there is no need to become agitated over the situation. However, what happens next depends on your reaction. Deal with the issue as soon as possible if it can be fixed and improved. Take a deep breath and let it go if you have no control over it.

THE FIRST FLINCH

The Stoics were aware that our first response to a circumstance is uncontrollable and cannot be avoided. They referred to it as "proto-passions." For example, suppose you've worked on a project for years for the government only to have it terminated by a new president. You're probably unhappy or dissatisfied right away. However, you have the choice whether or not to allow negative emotions to persist after the first instant of proto-passion. Our first response, maybe, is beyond our control, but we can manage how we respond to it. It's not what occurs initially that is important, but what you do afterwards. No matter what happens, you have the choice to fall back on your instincts or to rise above them and do what's best for yourself no matter what.

ADVERSITY IS AN ADVANTAGE

"I judge you unfortunate because you have never lived through misfortune. You have passed through life without an opponent— no one can ever know what you are capable of, not even you."
– Seneca, Letters From A Stoic.

The duality of control is essential to transforming an adverse circumstance into a positive one. It's out of your hands now, so don't worry about it. But you still have the power to decide how you respond. And the way you respond to the circumstance might be the difference between winning and losing.

Consider Richard Turner as an illustration of this. As a child, Richard suffered from scarlet fever. He became legally blind by the time he was an adolescent. The blindness didn't stop Richard from pursuing his life's ambitions. Instead, he took it as motivation to work harder. He achieved the rank of 5th Dan in the martial art of karate, became one of the best card magicians in history, and now as a magician for 14 hours a day, Richard hasn't missed an exercise in 40 years. How impressive is that?

Richard came to terms with the fact that he could do nothing to reverse his condition. There was, however, plenty that he could do about his situation. He opted to cope with the condition instead of feeling sorry for himself by working ten times harder than everyone else. Without sight, he has done more than most people with sight could ever hope to do.

Using the duality of control to transform misfortune into strength is the best thing you can do with the knowledge that you've gained. If you concentrate on what you can influence, you'll be at the top in no time.

HOW CAN THIS FIT INTO YOUR LIFE?

"Waste no more time arguing what a good man should be. Be one."

– Marcus Aurelius, Meditations 10:16

Philosophers 2,000 years ago were more than thinkers; they were doers. They never meant philosophy to be a purely intellectual pursuit; instead, it was a practical application of what one learns in the classroom. The term "philosophy" originally meant "love of wisdom," which is the application of knowledge. However, our generation has interpreted philosophy to mean "love of knowledge." Is your goal to study and use all you've learned like a contemporary philosopher or more like an old philosopher?

At the beginning of this chapter, I said that stoicism's duality of control is one of the most straightforward concepts. Yet, like with most things in life, simplicity does not equal ease. Although this concept is easy to grasp, putting it into action is where the rubber meets the road. You have to do the hard work if you want it to have a lasting impact on your life. You may apply this dichotomy in your own life in various ways:

- Prepare for difficulty

Preparing for challenges is a great way to practice stoicism. To improve your capacity to shrug off adversity, you'll need to visualize setbacks and failures. A flat tire, losing your wallet, being fired, or discovering that you have cancer are some things that you can imagine. Remember the duality of control when you see these challenges in your mind's eye; think about whether or not you can do something about them. This will help you practice categorizing things according to what you can control and what you can't. Take your time and be as descriptive as you can be while imagining these obstacles. Once you've done this a few times, you'll begin to view the world through the only two lenses that really count.

- Evening reflections

Spend 5 minutes every night before you go to bed reflecting on the events of the day. Take stock of what you could influence and what you couldn't. This is something Seneca did as well. Then, reflect on the moments when you let something outside of your control affect your feelings. Don't put yourself down for it, but accept what you might have done better and make it a goal for the future.

4

FACE IT HEAD ON

"Don't seek for everything to happen as you wish it would, but rather wish that everything happens as it actually will-then your life will flow well."
— Epictetus

Life ends in death. For all of us. Eventually. Death is the one certainty in life; everyone you know and love will die one day. As if that isn't bad enough, you'll have to deal with challenges throughout your life as you approach death.

Some of them will be pretty unpleasant. That's guaranteed. Whether you live for ten, fifty, or one hundred years doesn't matter. Like I stated in chapter one, stress is timeless. Every new chapter of your life will present you with one stressful situation or the other.

Fate has no mercy for anybody. There will be times in our lives when things won't go our way. We will risk losing our lives or having loved ones taken away. An accident could happen at any given time and change us for the rest of our lives. We could build things and have them unfairly taken away from us or watch them get destroyed. And these are just some of the possibilities in our reality.

Sadly, we have no power to stop all these things; all we can do is train ourselves to live well in such a world where terrible occurrences are not only possible, but should be expected. If we live in such a world, is it possible to find peace and joy? When faced with the harsh truths of life, many of us choose to bury our heads in the proverbial sand and pretend they don't exist. We hide until we are forced to face these situations head-on, and as a result, we are entirely unprepared to deal with them.

Although sorrow and disaster are inevitable, this is the worst conceivable way to live through life.

Stoicism offers us the skills necessary to have a peaceful and contented existence, regardless of how much sorrow and suffering we encounter or how long or short our lives wind up being.

The aspect of stoicism that particularly deals with this is known as stoic resilience. It is another aspect of stoicism that is truly simple to understand. The doctrine of stoic resilience revolves around the fact that we should enjoy what we have while it's ours, but also understand that these things never belong to us; we have no control over how long these things last; and the only difference between happiness and sadness lies in our perception of events, not the events themselves. As long as we can accomplish this, we will discover that pleasure and inner peace are achievable, no matter what script destiny has written for us.

Stoic resilience is the aspect of stoicism that helps us focus on our emotions. It helps us build our emotional resilience as it helps us easily adjust to hardship. It helps us toughen up mentally as people who are more emotionally resilient can better deal with the pressures of everyday life. This is what makes this doctrine so crucial for everyone. It doesn't matter whether you have just been through a rough patch in your life, if you're presently going through one, or if you are fortunate enough to be in a period of prosperity. I believe that stoic resilience is a quality that we can all benefit from at some point in our lives. The great thing about this stoic doctrine is that it is very practical.

HOW TO BECOME RESILIENT?

1. Become engaged in your daily activities

The ancient stoics made it a duty to live every day as their last. They were present in all their daily tasks because they knew that boredom could disturb our tranquility. When we are bored and restless, we are unable to relax. Restlessness interrupts our peacefulness and causes us to burden ourselves unnecessarily. We should aim to be like Seneca, who in "Letters From A Stoic" said, "I never spend a day in idleness; I appropriate even a part of the night for study."

How, then, do you deal with the monotony of life? All you need to do is be genuinely productive and engaged at work and home. I don't mean that you make sure you get results by being productive. What I'm saying is, be genuinely engaged in what you do both at home and work.

You'll find that you might not be as bored as you think you are. And yes, things may happen, and you may lose your work, or something else may come up that prevents you from making the most of your home as well. It doesn't matter; simply avoid giving up too quickly. No matter what comes your way, you should always look for another route if one is blocked, but always behave honorably. The goal is to be present and live genuinely.

2. Adapt to the circumstances of your life

We're used to the status quo, but life doesn't operate this way. You may sometimes find yourself in a bad situation. When that happens, keep in mind that you can still be happy in the worst of conditions; you merely need to adapt your behavior to the situation.

Stoics don't seek to answer every question; they adapt to situations. Epictetus taught in "The Discourses" that, "In this way, you must understand how laughable it is to say, 'Tell me what to do!' What advice could I possibly give? No, a far better request is, 'Train my mind to adapt to any circumstance."... In this way, if circumstances take you off script, you won't be desperate for a new prompting."

3. Do what you're capable of doing

"Because most of what we say and do is not essential. Ask yourself at every moment, 'Is this necessary?'"
-Marcus Aurelius, Meditations 4.24.

We tend to overestimate our capabilities. The reality is that there are some jobs that only certain people are equipped for, and you need to be conscious of that when you choose what to spend your time on. To discover whether you're up to the challenge, assess the work at hand. Try to stay away from work that is too difficult for you to finish, work that will only lead to more work, and work from which you have no way out, because unrealistic expectations lead to psychological pain.

4. Exercise caution while selecting friends

"If you consider any man a friend whom you do not trust as you trust yourself, you are mightily mistaken, and you do not sufficiently understand what true friendship means... When friendship is settled, you

must trust; before friendship is formed, you must pass judgment."
-Seneca, Letters From A Stoic.

There's nothing better than a long-term friend-ship that genuinely adds value to your life. The other side of that can be pretty draining. This is why you must make wise choices when choosing your social circle. However, don't hold out for the perfect companion. Good people are scarce, so make the best choice from the options presented. Be sure to run away from the sourpusses, or they'll bring you to their level.

5. Be Content

We tend to believe that we will be happy if we have all we desire. Because of this, we pursue money and material goods. However, this isn't the case. Just as Marcus Aurelius put it, "Very little is needed to make a happy life; it is all within yourself, in your way of thinking." Money is a poison that rots the soul. Those who lack it fear they will be deprived of it, while those who possess it fear losing it. The truth is, the best thing is to have just enough money to get by, rather than having an excessive desire for it. It doesn't mean you can't be ambitious, but know your priorities.

6. Rule over your cravings

Excessive indulgence is another factor contributing to our state of discontentment and the eventual loss of our tranquility. We worry about not having enough money all the time. However, even poverty could become riches if you exercise caution regarding spending. Live frugally. Avoid overt displays of wealth and ostentation. Even lovely things become unattractive if they are carried to their extremes.

7. Be a master of your destiny

We all have problems to deal with. They'll disrupt our peace of mind if we don't know how to handle them well. It is possible to overcome life's difficulties and maintain a peaceful mind if we work hard enough. As Marcus Aurelius said in Meditations 7.38, "You shouldn't give circumstances the power to rouse anger, for they don't care at all." Remember that they won't stay that way forever, no matter how bad things become. At first, it's tough to tolerate bad situations. After some time, though, they become tolerable. Don't burden others, yet be compassionate when things go wrong. We don't gain anything by remaining in that state of mind. The goal of a stoic is to move on and live in the present.

8. Avoid attachment to material things

If you're too tied to your possessions, you'll lose your peace of mind. Think of nothing as yours. Be ready to lose everything you possess at a moment's notice, even your own life, as the fear of death will only keep you from leading a meaningful life.

9. Cultivate the ability to foresee disaster

Even if you're a well-known person, things could change in the blink of an eye. Nothing is permanent, but you can overcome adversity and misfortune if you are prepared to face them. Be forewarned of bad luck and be ready for it. It is difficult to accept misfortune if you are ill-prepared when it occurs.

We can see this in the way Seneca lived his life. Writing to a friend, he said that "Nothing happens to the wise man against his expectation, nor do all things turn out for him as he wished but as he reckoned—and above all, he reckoned that something could block his plans."

10. Avoid busywork

Don't just do things for the sake of doing them. Avoid activities that serve a meaningless purpose at all costs. Many of us are preoccupied with the business of others. Eavesdropping and gossiping are excellent examples of meaningless activities you should avoid. Have a single purpose and focus all of your efforts on it and keep that goal in mind at all times.

11. Don't be surprised if you're let down

As a stoic, you're not just expected to prepare for disaster; you are to look forward to it. Seneca tells us, "what is quite unlooked for is more crushing in its effect, and unexpectedness adds to the weight of a disaster." There is wisdom in ensuring that nothing ever takes us by surprise. We should project our thoughts ahead of us at every turn and consider every possible eventuality instead of only the usual course of events. Rehearse them in your mind: exile, torture, war, shipwreck. "All the terms of our human lot should be before our eyes." Be prepared for things to go awry, even if you hope they will not. If things don't go according to plan, this will help alleviate the pain.

12. Do not be obstinate or indecisive

Keep an open mind, and don't get overly fixated on every little aspect of your goals. Things can and do change on a dime. Seneca encourages us to live by this principle, saying, "Whatever can happen at any time can happen today." Take it easy on yourself. Don't be surprised if things suddenly shift for the better or worse.

13. Take a lighthearted approach to life's challenges

Everything around us might make us feel hopeless at times. But it's better to laugh at human stupidity than to grieve it. Like Seneca said, "How does it help to make troubles heavier by bemoaning them?" Try to see things from a positive perspective. Even better, don't let yourself feel depressed or amused; instead, do what logic says and choose to be happy. Everything does not demand a reaction from you, especially negative things.

14. Embrace your fearlessness

Stoics are expected to be fearless, strengthened by the belief that it is unwise to worry about anything, especially things you cannot control. Seneca portrayed this principle by saying, "Wild animals run from the dangers they see, and once they have escaped them worry no more. We, however, are tormented alike by what is past and what is to come. Many of our blessings do us harm, for memory brings back the agony of fear while foresight brings it on prematurely. No one confines his unhappiness to the present." There are times when bad things happen even to the best of people. Cowards lament their misfortune, but bold people meet their challenges head-on. Let go of your sorrows. Embrace your adversity with a spirit of bravery.

15. Don't try to be someone you're not

Be yourself. Don't try to be someone you're not. People will have something negative to say about you no matter what you do. Spend time with friends and family and spend time alone - it will help you understand yourself better. Live as Marcus Aurelius did. He once wrote that "Whatever anyone does or says, I'm bound to the good. Whatever anyone does or says, I must be what I am and show my true colors."

16. Relax and enjoy yourself

To recharge, take a break. Stroll outside, attend a play or other kind of entertainment, and indulge in a drink or two. The key to a healthy lifestyle is moderation, also known as temperance - a stoic virtue. To keep your tranquility and recover it if lost, you can do things that help you relax, but you must be continuously on guard for them to be effective. (We will talk more about this in Chapter Six).

AMOR FATI

"Frightened of change? But what can exist without it? What's closer to nature's heart? Can you take a hot bath and leave the firewood as it was? Eat food without transforming it? Can any vital process take place without something being changed? Can't you see? It's just the same with you—and just as vital to nature."
- Marcus Aurelius, Meditations 7.18

There is no better way to maintain tranquility even while living in the present than to accept the present for what it is. This process of accepting what our present is is something the majority of the world struggles with, and which the stoics have dealt with using the concept of Amor Fati.

Amor Fati, or "love of destiny" or "love of one's fate," is one of several Stoic notions. We can easily say that accepting and embracing what has occurred, is occurring, and will happen is Amor Fati. It teaches us to be aware that change is a fact of life and that without it, we wouldn't be able to laugh or weep or love or create or develop.

Change is essential, regardless of how wonderful or terrible it is, how much fun or pain it brings. We are where we are now because of billions of years of ongoing change, variety, mutation, and development. Everything that has happened in your life has led to you reading this right now. As a result, we must learn to appreciate and accept our fates.

Living Amor Fati

What occurs to you in life is out of your hands, but you have power over how you react to it. This is the point of this philosophy, to accept responsibility for how we see and react to the world, not impose greater power over it,consciously choosing to improve our outlook on life. Amor Fati's approach is to help us change our perspective on what has or is occurring to us. For instance, if you've lost something, Amor Fati says that the situation has taught you to appreciate what you had and not take it for granted. Or were you laid off? Amor Fati asks, what previously closed doors did that open? When these events have already taken place, there is no advantage to being pessimistic about the future. It's impossible to change the past with negativity, but it is possible to improve our current lives with positivity.

Amor Fati as a theory of love

The Stoics are believed to have come up with the concept of Amor Fati, but over time, knowledge on the concept has evolved as it passed from generation to generation. Epictetus had his ideas about the subject. Marcus Aurelius also wrote about Amor Fati in his journal. Some later thinkers, like Friedrich Nietzsche, also used the phrase Amor Fati to express the idea of love in their works.

In the words of Nietzsche in his book "The Gay Science:" "My formula for greatness in a human being is Amor Fati: that one wants nothing to be different, not forward, not backward, not in all eternity. Not merely bear what is necessary, still less conceal it—all idealism is mendacity in the face of what is necessary—but love it." Nietzsche was trying to help us see that we shouldn't try to hide from our destiny, and we shouldn't wish it were otherwise. It's not what we want; it's what will be. It's time to deal with it. However, we should embrace and appreciate it rather than only accepting our destiny. Because whatever is going well for us now requires the whole universe and all of history to get to it. You wouldn't be here, and you wouldn't have had the joy you have if you didn't have that past.

That's why it's a bad idea to fight, despise, or grumble about your fate. Like dominoes falling on top of one other, the first domino must fall before the last can. For you to be here right now, all the circumstances of the past had to come together as they did. It's time to accept your destiny and use it for the greater good. Refusing to accept what has already occurred is a waste of time and energy.

Complaining is the enemy of doing

"If it is endurable, then endure it. Stop complaining."
-Marcus Aurelius, Meditations 10.3.

Wishing for anything different keeps us from embracing the world as it is, figuring out how to go ahead, and taking action. Complaining, winging it, and wishing for things to be different is almost always counterproductive. We imagine that we cannot do anything except wallow in self-loathing because things are as they are. But that is not true. Don't be afraid to take a chance on anything. The next time you're caught in the rain, remember this advice. Don't let the fact that you're wet get in the way of enjoying the experience. There are only so many years in a person's life, so why not make the most of them?

5

ARE YOU HERE?

"Each man only lives in this present instant...all the rest either has been lived or remains in uncertainty."
— **Marcus Aurelius, Debts and Lessons.**

This book is not about Buddhism, but philosophical studies are sometimes similar. It is expected that when a practitioner of one tradition encounters another, they take a moment to think about the similarities and distinctions between them - in this case, we'll consider a concept that has been associated with Buddhism, but that is not uniquely theirs. We are not doing this merely for the sake of doing it, though; we want to know how combining both studies can help us alleviate stress in our lives.

In their more modern 'engaged' and non-renunciant variants, both Stoicism and Buddhism are extremely pragmatic ideologies emphasizing the present moment, which we now know as mindfulness. Mindfulness is a concept that encourages us to be conscious that we are here, now, and that the only time to be alive is the present.

In light of this, it should come as no surprise that the Stoic concept of mindfulness occupies a fundamental position. *Prosoche*, the Greek word for "attention," is used by Epictetus in Discourses and Selected Writings to refer to the word mindfulness. "Even the seemingly minor activities of singing or playing may be done with prosoche," he tells his pupils in his lecture.

Epictetus believed that the concept of prosoche had a wide range of applicability in our lives. In his words, "Do you not realize that when once you have let your mind go wandering, it is no longer in your power to recall it, to bring it back to what is right, to self-respect, to moderation?" Although the concept of mindfulness in stoicism is not strictly practiced as it is in Buddhism, both philosophies agree that a well-directed mind will do us more service than any other thing in the world.

Although the Stoics didn't have practices like sitting meditation or focusing on the breath, their concept of mindfulness is still as effective in helping to reduce stress, anxiety, and worry. Now you might ask, if stoic mindfulness is not exactly like mindfulness, then what is it? Let's find out!

STOIC MINDFULNESS

In stoicism, mindfulness is referred to as "Prosoche." Prosoche is focused on developing the capacity to apply critical ethical principles to daily circumstances. It's about making sure you're focusing on what you can control rather than focusing on what you can't control—in other words, concentrating your efforts on becoming a good social being by controlling what you can manage.

In practicing prosoche, the most fundamental question to ask yourself is, "where am I in this situation? Is it something I can control or not?" The difference between the two may be imperceptible, yet the ramifications are significant. Let's take a look at a workplace scenario. Your manager's approval is something that is beyond your control, so if you position yourself to win her favor, you will be thrilled when she does and deflated when she doesn't. Your primary objective, in that case, is to get her approval. A Stoic would ask the question, "what is up to me in this situation?" instead of "what is up to others?"

"Within my control," for example, would mean concentrating on performing my work properly and peacefully. Even if the manager's opinion isn't up to me, it would be up to me to have a good working relationship with her. If the boss is delighted by that, it is good, but her approval is not the primary motivator for my efforts. I approached it as a craft in and of itself: I put in the time and effort to get the job done well. When it comes to performing one's craft, it's ironic that those who concentrate on the work at hand are more likely to succeed and receive the crowd's cheers.

Hence, "Where am I putting myself in this situation?" is a simple Stoic mindfulness exercise that you should ask yourself at different points during the day to evaluate how you're doing. Whenever your thoughts begin to 'invest' in things beyond your control, as Epictetus advised his pupils, remind yourself that "that has nothing to do with me!" One may compare this to subtle self-monitoring - a progressive increase in personal power in the direction of what you can accomplish and do effectively.

MINDFULNESS OR SELFISHNESS? WHAT'S THE DIFFERENCE?

It is also possible that Stoic mindfulness leads to a kind of selfishness, where you just care about your feelings and thoughts. But, this is not what the Stoics were aiming for. It's up to you as a logical and social creature to keep striving for the "good," a virtue and something that is inherently beneficial.

Like we said in the previous chapter, there is no "I" in me. Monitoring yourself and paying attention to your feelings so that you don't wind up stressing over things that are not within your control is not being selfish. You're merely becoming mindful of yourself.

Although "Me" and "Mine" are generally seen as problematic in Buddhism since they lead to a desire for possessions and a sense of self-importance, stoicism does not have an issue with the use of "Me" and "Mine," provided that these terms are used to refer to what is under one's control and one's desire to do good.

This is how Epictetus describes it in "The Discourses:" "For where one can say 'I' and 'mine,' to there will the human being incline. If 'I' and 'mine' are placed in the flesh, there will the human being's ruling power be; if they are in the moral purpose, there must it be; if they are in externals, there must it be; If, therefore, I am where my moral purpose is, then, and then only, will I be the friend and son and father that I should be. For then this will be of interest – to keep my good faith, my self-respect, my forbearance, my co-cooperation, and to maintain my relationships with other human beings."

Stoicism aims to gradually replace the selfish ego with a more benevolent one. Kindness, generosity, and philanthropy are qualities that are "up to me." It's because of stoic observations of nature that this is the case. For the stoics, human beings were innately designed for cooperation, living in groups, and raising families. So, if we're going to live up to our social nature, we have to show compassion and care for others.

Living as a social being can be quite demanding on us physically and mentally, but mindfulness helps us achieve balance. It helps remove the stress of needing to please others, which is one of the most prominent stressors today. To practice mindfulness the stoic way, you don't need much. You just have to evaluate where you stand in every situation by asking yourself if it is one that you can control or not, and ensuring that you do what is right to the best of your ability.

Yet there is more to the Stoic concept of "up to us." With stoic mindfulness, even though you concentrate on what you can control in any given scenario, you must execute it skillfully and with consideration for others. Now you can see that even the notion of a "community of humans" has its roots in stoicism. As Seneca, in "Letters From A Stoic," put it: "No philosophy is kinder or more lenient, more philanthropic or attentive to the common good."

6

THE SQUARE OF VIRTUES

"To bear trials with a calm mind robs misfortune of its strength and burden."
— **Seneca, Letters From A Stoic.**

I n all my years of practicing stoicism, in my interactions with fellow stoics on alleviating stress, being mindful of yourself, and remaining in the good, I have observed that we all have questions. Sometimes these questions are so mind-blowing that I am left to wonder and search through various philosophical topics to find the answers, even with my in-depth knowledge of stoicism.

Yet, in all these interactions, I have found that many people wonder about one thing in particular: What should my course of action be in this particular scenario? Or what should a stoic do under these circumstances? I am certain that the ancient stoics also had to answer these questions, which is why they created a moral compass. What is this moral compass? It is known as the four stoic virtues: Wisdom, Courage, Justice, and Temperance.

In times of adversity, perplexity, and ordinary life, the ancient Stoics relied on these four qualities as a compass to guide their conduct. To them, morality is the key to contentment. The stoics believed that happiness comes from living ethical lives in harmony with nature.

THE FOUR STOIC VIRTUES

1. The virtue of wisdom

Wisdom is the capacity to distinguish between right, wrong, and neutral. For instance, Right: Demonstrating bravery and moderation in the face of anxiety or cravings for excessive indulgence. Wrong: Lying to escape responsibilities, choosing sloth, greed, and unhealthy habits in-

STOICISM FOR STRESS RELIEF

stead of moderation and restraint, and taking advantage of others or the community to gain an edge over them. Neutral: Money, possessions, celebrity, etc.

The Stoics held that virtue and vice are mutually exclusive. Virtue brings us closer to happiness, while vice drives us away. Wisdom is just the capacity to distinguish between right and wrong, which allows us to make more careful decisions about our actions. Yet the stoics prefer indifference. Things like money, riches, and fame were considered indifferents by the Stoics, who saw them as unimportant. They did not assign a moral charge to them; these things just exist.

Stoicism goes a little further to say that it's possible to prefer items that aren't very special. Poverty can't compare with being rich and good health can't compare with being sick. The truth is that these things are neither good nor evil. It is a person's actions and purpose that make them good or bad.

2. The virtue of courage

"There are misfortunes which strike the sage – without incapacitating him, of course – such as physical pain,

infirmity, the loss of friends or children, or the catastrophes of his country when it is devastated by war. I grant that he is sensitive to these things, for we do not attribute the hardness of a rock or iron to him. There is no virtue in putting up with that which one does not feel."
-Seneca, Letters From A Stoic.

Courage is the antithesis of cowardice. It is not the eradication of fear, desire, and worry; it is only the proper way to deal with them. Someone who doesn't experience fear isn't courageous since they can't overcome it. Courage is the ability to overcome one's insecurities. In other words, it means doing the right thing even if we're terrified to do so.

The tale of a Stoic instructor caught in a violent storm on a boat dates back millennia. In this story, a violent storm started to lash at the ship's hull and sails as it sailed over the Ionian Sea. The ship began filling with water as the waves rose higher.

One of the travelers was an Athens-based Stoic instructor. During the storm, his face went white, and he had a terrified expression on his face. Shortly after that, when the waves had calmed, a

STOICISM FOR STRESS RELIEF

passenger came to ask the philosopher why his face went pale during the storm while he (the passenger) felt no fear.

Because of his condescending demeanor, the Stoic brushed the guy aside. Another passenger then approached the Stoic later in the trip and politely inquired about the source of his apprehension. Because of his interest, the stoic approached him differently. He provided him with a portion of Epictetus' The Enchiridion. Specific to fear, in this case.

According to Epictetus in this book, it's impossible to escape the first phases of dread. When a building or a ship is in danger of collapsing, our first instinct is to worry and feel terrified, which can cause us to lose rationality and clarity of cognition. According to Epictetus, a sensible man does not give credence to such irrational thoughts. These impulses are wrong as far as Epictetus was concerned.

In his words; "But the wise man, after being affected for a short time and slightly in his color and expression, 'does not assent,' but retains the steadfastness and strength of the opinion which he has always had about visions of this kind, namely that they are in no wise to be feared but excite terror by a false appearance and vain alarms." His point? Having the strength of character and morality even when we would rather not is what we mean when we say that we have courage.

3. The virtue of justice

The stoic concept of justice is far larger than the concept of justice in our legal and linguistic systems today. According to the Stoics, Justice is a responsibility we owe to our fellow man and our community. In other words, it's the code of conduct that guides our behavior toward one another and the other members of our community.

To quote Cicero, "Justice is the crowning glory of all virtues." If justice is your moral compass, it guides the other virtues. It helps you concentrate your efforts on the greater good rather than your own interests. Just as Marcus Aurelius said in Debts and Lessons, "That which is not good for the bee-hive cannot be good for the bee," hence if we harm the people around us, we harm ourselves.

4. The virtue of temperance

Moderation is another name for temperance. It has to do with self-control, self-restraint, and self-discipline. It's about choosing long-term well-being rather than short-term pleasure. As the saying goes, when pleasure exceeds a certain point, it becomes punishment. Gluttony, greed, the need for immediate satisfaction, addictive behavior, sloth, and procrastination are all antithetical to the concept of temperance and self-control.

The virtue of moderation allows us to separate our well-being from vices like materialism, alcohol, drugs, social media, video games, and pornography. To be clear, I'm not advocating that you pack up your belongings and go to the mountains to herd goats. I am saying that enjoying yourself in moderation is generally a good idea. We fail to see how needless some things are until we have learned to do without them.

STOIC VIRTUES AS A MORAL COMPASS

To determine how to deal with stressful situations and decide what is good for us and others, we can let the stoic virtues be our guide. Despite our doubts and worries, they give us the courage that leads us to do the right thing. To keep our minds from succumbing to the temptations of addiction, sloth, and greed, we get temperance from them. Justice serves as a catalyst for behavior that benefits the whole community. Finally, we have wisdom, the quality that enables us to distinguish between good and bad in the world.

Do not take on these virtues at once when implementing them to guide your decisions. Seek each of them out one after the other. Remember that what works for one person may not work for another. Stoics have relied on these pillars for thousands of years to guide their activities. They're certainly a great starting point for you and me. They are also most essential to us because sometimes, when dealing with stress, you will feel selfish. These virtues will help guide you on handling situations, not just for your own good, but for the greater good.

7

HABITUATE YOUR PEACE

"Every habit and capability is confirmed and grows in its corresponding actions, walking by walking, and running by running . . . therefore, if you want to do something, make a habit of it."
— **Epictetus, The Enchiridion.**

Anything worth doing in life, if you want to do it well, requires consistency. According to Epictetus, if you want to change the course of your life, pick one thing and make it a habit, then be consistent with it. The Stoics highly valued habits and rituals. Marcus Aurelius had a morning routine that was a form of preparation for the day. One story has it that Marcus' stepfather Antoninus Pius, who served as both his mentor and stepfather, was very strict about how much time he spent in the toilet to get more work done and help more people.

We know that the Stoics were big on routine. Although their styles were unique, they had to have a routine. We need routines too. This is true for just about every career, or aspiration. To have a more fulfilling life, you need repetition and habit. Great work and good judgments don't happen by accident—at least, not regularly.

I cannot overstate the importance of following a schedule. If you want to live a stress-free life, you have to be committed to it. And although there is no singular handbook that offers a complete guide on how to live a stress-free life, stoicism offers some helpful strategies if you wish to acquire inner calmness.

1. Negative visualization

When you expect that anything in your life, or a certain component of it, will turn out well, you are putting yourself at risk of disappointment. That's why many people have a good attitude in the morning and a bad attitude at the end of the day.

The Stoics used "negative visualization" to combat the unpleasantness of life's situations. When you're pessimistic, you're really preparing yourself for unpleasant and uncomfortable circumstances by seeing them in your mind. This was the reasoning behind Marcus Aurelius' statement, "Begin each day by telling yourself: Today I shall be meeting with interference, ingratitude, insolence, disloyalty, ill-will, and selfishness – all of them due to the offenders' ignorance of what is good or evil." When Marcus Aurelius used a combination of negative visualization and a positive outlook to regulate his expectations, he protected his spirit from harm.

2. Practice self-control

Being able to regulate your impulses and keep away from addictive behavior will be quite helpful in focusing on the things that are important to you. As you know, according to the Stoics, there are two categories of things in life: those we can influence and those we cannot influence. Epictetus once stated in "The Discourses": "Things in our control are opinion, pursuit, desire, aversion, and in a word, whatever are our own actions. Things not in our control are body, property, reputation, command and in one word, whatever are not our own actions."

The most important thing is to focus on what we can control, which requires practice. You can do this in several ways. For instance, for you, it could be that it's hard to resist temptation when it comes to eating. You could start controlling that by practicing intermittent fasting, where you don't eat for a certain period.

3. Keep a Journal

Writing down your ideas helps you find comfort and organize your memories and thoughts. As a result, writing has a calming impact on the brain. Marcus Aurelius had a diary. This diary later got published as a book and is one of the major sources of stoic wisdom to this day. Epictetus and Seneca kept journals of their own. Seneca had this to say in "Letters From A Stoic:" "When the light has been removed, and my wife has fallen silent, aware of this habit that's now mine, I examine my entire day and go back over what I've done and said, hiding nothing from myself, passing nothing by."

In stoicism, journaling is considered to be one of the most impactful activities one could do. It was so useful because they journaled the right way. Don't just write down the events of the day - journal your thoughts and the lessons you learned from those events.

4. Remember death

Keep in mind that you're a mortal! Memento mori is the act of consciously reminding yourself that one day, we will all die. It is a reminder that time passes quickly and that we should not squander it on frivolous pursuits. It reminds us that today may be our last day on Earth, so we should enjoy it to the fullest. The stoics believed that we should not be afraid of death, but instead be grateful for the life that we have been given. Seneca said of death, "let us prepare our minds as if we'd come to the very end of life. Let us postpone nothing. Let us balance life's books each day. The one who puts the finishing touches on their life each day is never short of time."

5. Consider yourself in the grand scheme of things

Let's work with the commonly accepted view that the Earth is a sphere, regardless of whether some people think it is flat. This orb is a little speck in our solar system compared to Jupiter and Saturn. Now imagine that the sun, which, compared to the many, many other galaxies that make up the Milky Way, is very small. You will be able to let go of many trivialities when you recognize how little you really are. From a cosmic perspective, the irritating colleague, the mother-in-law, and the person who cut you off in traffic are not so relevant. Large events like wars and natural catastrophes are trivial compared to the enormity of the universe. Our smallness is humbling and puts our existence in perspective. Sometimes perspective will make you laugh at those who get triggered and outraged by foolish, meaningless things.

6. Accept your fate and love it

When we worry, we want the future to look a certain way and hate the thought of things turning out different. Worrying about the future is a common problem for many people, but the Stoics had a simple remedy for it: Amor Fati, "Love of Fate." It teaches you that you'll be okay no matter what occurs in your life as long as you accept the result.

Although we have considered the subject of Amor Fati before, it is important that you don't just see it as a philosophical concept, but as some-thing you can implement in your day-to-day life. Don't get it wrong, Amor Fati does not imply that we should become cynical and do nothing. The idea is that you don't become attached to the re-sult, but enjoy the process.

AFTERWORD

Some things are integrally part of the human experience and stress is one of them. Understandably, though, when things get too real you start to long for a simpler time. As I have shown you in this book, that desire is pointless. Why would you obsess over things you cannot control? No matter how hard you wish it away, stress will be an unwelcome companion in life.

What is yours to control, though, is how you see things. You have the power to choose your perspective. You have the option to respond to life's pressures in a sensible and intelligent manner, and thanks to this book, flourish in the face of adversity. Here, you've learned the Stoic's finest methods for coping with stress and worry. Are you going to use them?

Amor Fati!

THANK YOU!

Thank you so much for buying my book.

I know you had many options to pick from but you picked this one.

Because of that, I am grateful. Thank you for reading it to the end. I hope that you have gotten what you came here for and then some.

Before you go, I need to ask for a small favor from you. **Would you kindly post a review of the book? Leaving a review is the easiest and best way to support our work.**

And you know what? Your feedback helps me to keep writing books like this one that will hold

your hand toward the kind of personal changes you want to make in your life. It would mean the world to me to hear from you.

ALSO BY ALEXANDER CLARKE

Visit my author page

author.to/alexanderclarke

STOP OVER THINKING

The 34 Best Techniques to Reducing Stress,
Controlling Your Mind, Overcoming Negative
Thoughts and Living a Worry-Free Life

ALEXANDER CLARKE

YOUR FREE GUIDE

To help you control your mind I've created a guide with 9 easy tools from Stoics to build mental strength. Make sure you download it at the following URL:

alexander-clarke.com

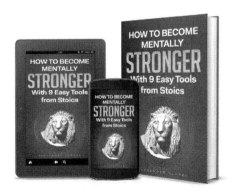

It will help you greatly on your personal development journey. The stronger you train your mind to be, the more you will control your thoughts.

If you want to master your mind and your emotions make sure to grab this free guide!

REFERENCES

Aurelius, M. (2006). *Meditations.* Penguin Books.

Epictetus. (1995). *The Discourses .* Everyman.

Irvine, W. B. (2009). *Stoicism: A Guide To The Good Life.* Oxford University Press.

Lake, G. (2013). *From Stress to Stillness .* Endless Satsang Foundation .

Sellar, J. (2006). *Stoicism.* Acumen.

Seneca. (2004). *Letters From A Stoic.* Penguin Books.

Weaver, T. (2020, January 22nd). Retrieved from Orion Philosophy https://www.orionphilosophy.com/

THE POWER OF STOICISM

24 STOIC LESSONS TO LIVE HAPPIER, CARE LESS, MASTER YOUR EMOTIONS & BECOME UNSHAKABLE LIKE A STOIC

or indirect, which are incurred as a result of the use of the information contained within this document, including, but not limited to, — errors, omissions, or inaccuracies.

YOUR FREE GUIDE

To help you control your mind I've created a guide with 9 easy tools from Stoics to build mental strength. Make sure you download it at the following URL:

alexander-clarke.com

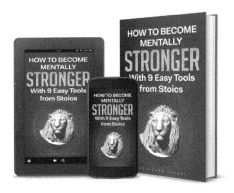

It will help you greatly on your personal development journey. The stronger you train your mind to be, the more you will control your thoughts.

If you want to master your mind and your emotions make sure to grab this free guide!

ALSO BY ALEXANDER CLARKE

Visit my author page

author.to/alexanderclarke

STOP OVER THINKING

The 34 Best Techniques to Reducing Stress,
Controlling Your Mind, Overcoming Negative
Thoughts and Living a Worry-Free Life

ALEXANDER CLARKE

INTRODUCTION

'Begin to live at once, and consider each separate day a separate life. He who has prepared himself that way, whose life every day is a rounded whole, is easy in his mind.' – **Seneca.**

When Seneca wrote about considering each day a separate life, he had just finished telling his friend about someone he knew who had built his life from rags to riches. Seneca's acquaintance had spent most of his life working to move from poverty to prestige and was just beginning to see the fruit of his labors when he suddenly died. The first time I heard this story, it hit me that nothing in life is promised. We live within the bounds of our mortality. It occurred to me that it is a foolish thing to be reckless and assume that we have all the time to make grand plans for the excellent life we will eventually live. I don't know about you but for the longest time, whenever a new year began, I would make grand plans for a distant future. In the best year, only about one of those plans became a reality.

What I didn't realize is that even though there is value in aiming life in a general direction and creating specific goals and plans, unless those become daily habits, it's all work in vain. That is because the way we spend our days is how we spend our lives. Seneca went on to advise that the better approach to life is to make grand plans for a quality day – make every day count. The idea? If you string together enough quality days and you live them well, then you will have a great year and a great life. I found that idea mind-blowing. But it did not produce the change I hoped in my life. Not yet anyway. I was still unsatisfied and unhappy with my life. That knowledge was still a rumor because it was yet to enter my body.

When I was young, it seemed like people treated their ideas like accessories for a social persona. If you were an anarchist, for example, like one teenage boy I remember meeting, then that was a fashion statement. Whatever the idea, to me it seemed like it was only a label – something superficial. Of course, I did not think of life in those terms. I was too young and inarticulate, but I knew I was indifferent to those things. I was simply not interested in labels. Maybe I sensed that most of it was posturing. Whatever the case, I decided to start reading old books. I figured that if I read stuff written many decades ago, the perspective would be genuinely different. It would transcend the socially acceptable.

During that period, I stumbled upon Marcus Aurelius' *Meditations* and it opened a whole new world to me. Something about the book resonated with me. I learned about philosophy and read up on the stoics. I took in everything I could and of course, as if unwittingly, my life changed and took a form I had always desired but one that had been out of reach until then. Stoicism became a guiding star to me. It became my survival guide. Back then, one of the hallmarks of my life was lack of emotional control. My emotions always swayed my decisions, and never in the right direction. I was an emotional hazard sign, except, I was not regulated by any human law, societal expectation, or my conscience. Something had to give. There had to be a way to deal with all the anger, sadness, pressure, anxiety, and fear. There had to be a solution to all my suffering. There had to be peace.

You see, every one of us has within our brain an encyclopedia – a library, even – of information. We hold many experiences, lessons, and observations which form our thoughts, beliefs, and values. Some of this information is fact and some of it is generalizations, assumptions, and ideas we hold because we trust the people who told us. It follows that not all our beliefs support our well-being. Yet, some of us go through life never questioning what we believe and never intentionally working to improve our lives. Embracing stoicism is bringing those beliefs to the conscious mind and choosing what you will believe and live by. It is dipping a fork into the complex soup of perspectives and ideas in your mind and disposing of what you do not need.

If this sounds a bit complex, maybe some stoics will explain it better. Marcus Aurelius once said that the soul is dyed with the color of its thoughts. Another stoic, Epictetus, added that men are only disturbed by things because of the way they see them. The stoics picked up on a human thread. They understood how much control our minds have on the way we live. Our minds are to our lives what the camera is to the quality of a picture. A dirty lens equals a poor image. A mind filled with negative beliefs produces suffering. The stories we live out and the beliefs we hold dear affect how we experience life.

Fortunately, we have the power to change what we believe and in so doing, change what we experience. We have, from the generous library of stoic writings, the collection of knowledge we need to get closer to living a good life. At any moment and in any situation or stage of life, stoicism offers a framework to live well. It reminds us of what truly matters and provides practical strategies to do more of what is valuable. Stoicism as a philosophy was deliberately designed to be actionable, understandable, and useful so that you do not need to learn a new philosophical language to practice stoicism. It offers an immediate and practical way to find peace and improve your strength of character.

This book is for you if you know what it is like to be unsatisfied with the life you are living. It is for you if you dislike having negative thinking and negative emotions control you. Here, you will learn how to deal with the big life emotions. You will understand how anger can be your friend. You will discover how you can make use of your anxiety, fear, and sadness. In this book, you will see how the wise men of old managed their lives and what principles and ideas led them to have as much influence as they did. Hopefully, by the end of this book, you will no longer let your emotions control how you behave and how you experience life.

Perhaps your biggest concern is not so much that your emotions control your decision, but that they seem to steal your peace. Maybe whenever you chart a course in life, anxiety steals your peace of mind. This book also has something for you. You will understand how to stop worrying about things you cannot control. You will learn how to focus on what is yours to change. Depression and anxiety will no longer rule you - and when you face setbacks, rather than caving and giving up, you will learn how to find the strength to move forward, beyond the setback into the space you want to be in. You will do this with such mental balance and clarity it will astound you.

By the end of this book, you will be able to distinguish between what is a story and what is real. Most of the time, when our beliefs and the stories we embrace become inflexible, and when we blur the line between story and reality, we suffer. These inflexible stories leave no room for contradicting evidence, causing us to become irritable, defensive, irrational, and intolerant. After going through this book, your beliefs will no longer be inflexible. You will learn to be fluid – to roll with the punches, if you will. But this book will also demand something from you. It will demand a willingness to examine yourself. It is your individual responsibility to look at what you believe and make sure it is serving you, not getting in your way.

When I started reading about stoicism, I found a lot of the books about it unhelpful. Most of them were either too broad, too complex, or too academic to be of practical help. Others were simply too much for someone new to stoicism or read like a fluffy self-help book. I have worked to make this book different. My passion for stoicism has not only brought me here, to writing this book, but it has also made it that I have designed every chapter and every part to help you implement real stoicism in your life. The advice you find here is practical and adapted to our modern world and life struggles. By design, this book has very deep roots in traditional stoicism, but it is also intentionally contemporary. One of my goals with writing books like this is to be part of the renaissance of stoic ideas. I hope for a future that includes being able to impact and change the lives of millions through my work, to help you live a happier life and better control your mind.

Other than my avid love for stoicism, I also hold a BA in Behavioral Psychology and an MA in Philosophy, qualifications which greatly inform how I apply stoicism to modern life challenges. I have worked as a coach and counselor for many years and I have had the privilege of guiding many of my clients in their journey to integrate stoicism into their lives. I have watched how stoic ideas have revolutionized their thinking and their lives and I am excited to do the same with this book. I currently live in North Carolina with the love of my life, two children, and a dog. I have managed to do things I never thought I would ever do with my life. I have traveled widely. I have even climbed Mount Kilimanjaro in Tanzania and Denali in Alaska and I look forward to other awesome adventures in my life. These things have only been possible because of the stoic ideas I will discuss in this book. In a lot of ways, I owe them to the discovery of Marcus Aurelius' *Meditations*. You'll do well to take them to heart and to live them out.

I have divided this book into four parts. The *first part* is about achieving happiness through virtue and discipline. You will shift from a self-indulgent and near-sighted pursuit for happiness as the end result of all your efforts to a pursuit of discipline and virtue that produces happiness as a fruit. *Part two* talks about mastering your emotions. Here, you will see how the stoics dealt with theirs and how their wisdom can help you today. *Part three* will help you to care less. It will allow you to harness the power of indifference and *part four* will help you to master your mind. My goal is to provide a lasting answer to your pain by dealing with the things that cause your suffering. If this sounds like why you are here, keep reading!

PART I

ACHIEVING HAPPINESS THROUGH DISCIPLINE AND VIRTUE

1

HOW TO BE A STOIC LIKE EPICTETUS - WHAT CAN YOU CONTROL?

'No great thing is created suddenly, any more than a bunch of grapes. If you tell me that you want grapes, I answer that there must be time. Let the grave vine blossom, then bear fruit, then ripen.'
– Epictetus.

Today, you can practice stoicism to different degrees. Some people say that you have to become stoic and live your life as they did, to the tiniest detail. That is one way to go, but I have found that it is not the only way. You can benefit from stoicism without following it religiously. You can apply the stoics' rational, practical, and logical wisdom to situations you find distressing, the same way you use a bandage when you are wounded. As you regularly and repeatedly do this, your reactions to life events begin to change. Soon enough, you apply stoicism on autopilot – it becomes your portable philosophical first aid kit. That is what this first chapter is about – helping you learn how to start using stoicism in your life.

According to the philosophy, the key to a good and happy life is to cultivate an excellent mental state, which some stoics associated with being rational and virtuous. To them, you live the ideal life if you are in harmony with nature and have an attitude of indifference toward the external. The philosophy started in Greece around 300 BC with Zeno. Zeno of Citium used to teach at a place in Athens with a Painted Stoa, hence the name – stoicism.

There are many ways to understand the practice of stoicism because it is an ancient philosophy. The philosophy developed for over five centuries - from Zeno all the way to Marcus Aurelius. Epictetus and his famous three disciplines – desire, action, and assent, is one of the traditional ways of approaching the philosophy. We will explore the things he believed about life and our interaction with it – how to deal with frustration and anxiety. Then, at the end of the chapter, we will apply his ideas to modern living to give you a basic foundation of stoic philosophy.

Meet Epictetus.

Epictetus was born around 55AD as a slave in Hierapolis – present-day Pamukkale in Turkey. The first time I came across his teachings, I lived alone, had just joined campus, and I was dealing with a troubled long-distance relationship. I was demoralized and disillusioned by politics. I felt a lot like a victim. The first line in Epictetus' *The Enchiridion* made me feel like some weight had been lifted off me. He starts the book by saying, 'some things are in our control, and others are not.' For him, the only thing that we can fully control, and the only thing that we should worry about if we must worry, is our judgment about right and wrong.

Epictetus explains that if you desire reputation, sex, health, or money, you will inevitably become unhappy. Anyone who wishes to avoid loneliness, obscurity, sickness, and poverty will live in constant frustration and anxiety. He does not pretend that you can live without desire or fear. They are unavoidable. Everyone feels those human flashes of anticipation or dread. Being stoic is about interrogating the flashes to see if they apply to the things you cannot control. If they do, then your response should be, 'that is not my concern.'

Think about your life and your anxieties. You will find, like I did, that most of the pain in your life does not come from actual loneliness, sickness, or trouble, but from the shame you experience thinking that it could have been avoided. Is it your fault that your job is demanding, for example? What is the source of your shame? Epictetus was the slave of a man named Epaphroditus. His master allowed him to pursue liberal studies, which is how he discovered Musonius Rufus, the stoic who became his mentor and teacher. Later on, he gained his freedom and began teaching philosophy. He kept teaching philosophy until his death, even when his life changed because of the political climate at the time. It is the tight grip on the limits of his control that kept him going.

After his death, someone bought his earthenware lamp for a lot of money. It is said that he kept his lamp next to his household gods. It was the lamp that had once been stolen and taught him a valuable life lesson. He learned, from the theft, that a man loses only what he already possesses. This lesson became the guiding lamp for his life. His work now provides a framework for enduring trouble in life, which is fitting because the man had a disabled leg, probably broken by his master when he was a slave. As far as Epictetus was concerned, sickness only hinders your body, not your ability to make decisions.

EPICTETUS ON TODAY'S WORLD

Whenever you find yourself in a fix, whether it is sickness or an obstacle to your plans, tell yourself that the obstacle only gets in your way if you let it.

Remind yourself of what you can control - Desire

In his work, *The Enchiridion*, Epictetus begins with a maxim that has become a pillar of stoic philosophy. He asks the question – what is within your control? According to Epictetus, it is noble to want/desire only what is within your control. Do not get upset or angry at things you cannot influence, whether they be external events or other people. Instead, focus on your behavior. This attitude will help you to let go and accept things as they are. At the same time, it will empower you to control what you can. As the man said, we can control our opinions, aversions, desires, and actions. We cannot control our property, reputation, body, or other people's actions.

Set a standard - Action

It is a universal truth that people with influence, the real leaders, no matter the sphere of life, rarely talk of the way things should be done. It is their actions that show it. Think of someone you admire – how many things did they tell you, and how many did you learn from their choices? To be a stoic like Epictetus, focus on how you live and your choices/actions. Live out, rather than, talk about your standard. That is where you will spend your energy and time best. Be like Epictetus; never be content with theorems that do not govern your life.

Prescribe a character for yourself - Assent

Epictetus knew that a lot of our actions are guided by habit, and that we tend to think that our habits cannot be changed. He encouraged his students to come up with standards and principles that they would follow as they went through life. This is a good idea for anyone beginning their interaction with stoicism. Do not imagine that it will be easy, but prescribing yourself a character and making small steps every day toward that direction will get you closer to who you want to be. Pertaining to this book, that character is a resolve to use the tried and tested stoic wisdom in your moments of distress.

~

What can you control?

With the three steps in this chapter, you can begin your journey of integrating stoicism into your life. You can start letting the grapevine blossom and bear fruit. So far, we have seen that:

- Life inevitably will have things that are out of your control.
- You will be most effective if you only focus on what you can control.
- Having a standard and a character will keep you on the right path.

In the next chapter, we will explore the three pillars of stoicism so that you can better understand what you are signing up for.

2

THE THREE PILLARS OF STOICISM EXPLAINED - PURSUE VIRTUE

'Oh, ye who have learnt the doctrines of the Stoa, and committed to your divine books, the best human learning, teaching men that virtue is the only good! She is the only one who keeps the lives and cities of men safer than walls and gates. Those who place their happiness in pleasure, are led by the least worthy muse.'
– Athenaeus the Epigrammatist as quoted by Diogenes.

When most people talk about stoicism, they talk about the practical guidelines for life, which is good. I have designed this book to take that form because, really, what is the use of theory if you cannot practice it? But for Zeno the Citium, the founder of the philosophy, the question was not simply how to live. He thought that you could understand life from other deeply philosophical questions, and so he divided the philosophy into three areas, which came to be known as the pillars of stoicism–ethics, physics, and logic.

He thought of physics as pertaining to the universe and its nature. Zeno and the stoics believed the universe was a divine entity, so when they referred to physics, they meant investigating the divine and the natural. The second pillar pertains to logos. For him, logic is how we think of the world, both as individuals and as a society. It includes disciplines like grammar, rhetoric, perception, and so forth. The stoics believed that the world is underpinned by reason – logic is a kind of fire under the universe. They argued that logic must be part of the material nature of the world, which is why you can think of the cosmos as divine. For the stoics, God was the creative and productive part of the unfolding cosmos.

The final pillar encompasses ethics and the practical questions about how to live. This is the part we talk about a lot. Even though this book seeks to make every chapter practical, I have not disregarded the physics and logos of stoicism. The stoic ideal is to live as one with nature, and set your expectations so that you are not pushing against nature. It is living in accordance with nature. Before applying the three pillars to your life, let's first discuss them in depth:

Understanding logic

Most of the time, we take our rational thinking for granted. We disregard the cause-and-effect law associated with our thoughts even though the past has proven that human thinking does not work that way. Then, there is the whole spectrum of people who are entirely directed by their emotions. The stoics did not believe in living a life led by emotions. Rather, they bowed to logic. They thought of logic as an art form. No wonder they worked hard to develop their minds. Diogenes, talking about stoic logic, wrote: 'The wise man must always love dialect. Everything is seen once you consider it in arguments. Through debate, you understand what belongs to the ethos and what belongs to physics.'

Think of logic as the hard shell that encompasses physics and ethics. It is the solid and firm art of logic that you have to master so that you can enjoy and benefit from the other aspects of stoicism. The philosophy is based on some rules of language. For example, if you are in your house during the day and look out of your window, it is light outside. You can say confidently that *'it is light.'* If it really is during the day, then your conclusion is true, but if it is night, then your conclusion is false. According to the stoics, rules like this govern the world. They make the logos. They are natural principles of existence.

Unpacking ethics

Ethics is about the things that are appropriate to do and those that are not. The argument of the stoics is that after you master the logos, then you can start mastering the ethics. They divided ethics into two – virtue and vice. Virtue will always contribute to your happiness while vice will birth misery. They went on to divide virtue and vice into other classifications that we will discuss later in this book. However, between virtue and vice, there is an expansive gray area where things are neither good nor bad – they are morally neutral.

The stoics called the things that are morally neutral, indifferents. You can do something within this gray area, and the context will determine whether it is moral or immoral. It is the ability to reason that helps you make that distinction and to decide how you should proceed. Essentially, indifferents will not harm or contribute toward your happiness. It is how you use them that will affect your happiness. But how do you use them? Zeno thought that the point of life is to move smoothly along the natural course of things. He considered everything to be part of one system that he called 'nature.' A good life harmonizes with that nature.

Virtue is when everything you are doing agrees with nature. Conversely, vice is when what you are doing disagrees with nature. When it comes to the indifferents, the stoics differentiated between dispreferred and preferred indifferents. Strength, pleasure, and wealth, for example, are preferred indifferents. They make our natural condition positive, but it is not guaranteed that they will lead to happiness. Dispreferred indifferents are things like poverty, ugliness, weakness, and disease. They make our natural condition a little worse, but they only cause misery if you let them. How you use either of the indifferents is what determines whether or not you live a happy life.

It all starts with physics

You cannot live in accordance with nature if you do not understand it. When the stoics talked about physics, they meant nature. It is not to be confused with what we call physics in the modern world. Stoic physics is about understanding the universe. The stoics' understanding of the universe was very complex, so I will only introduce the basics. They believed in a divine entity they called the logos, the force behind reason. According to them, we exist in two levels – pneuma and matter. Matter is everything that we can perceive with our senses. It is lifeless, destroyable, and passive.

Pneuma is the active force that moves the cosmos. It is fully integrated with matter, but it cannot be destroyed. Some stoics thought of the pneuma as the vehicle for the logos. It is what lends life to the universe. It propels the waves of the sea, the movement of the planets and stars, and even the existence of life itself. The stoics maintained that life was already predetermined. They thought that there are many realities, all of which are predetermined. You play out the reality that corresponds with your choices. This is to say that the choices you make determine your path.

It is understandable if this sounds very complicated. Some scholars considered the interaction of the three pillars of stoicism as some sort of egg. The egg yolk represents physics, ethics is the egg white, and logic is the shell. These scholars say that physics drives stoicism. They argue that if you do not know how the universe works, then you cannot determine what is good or bad. I have found that these pillars are more interdependent. Without one, the whole system will collapse.

Are you pursuing virtue?

For the stoics, there is no happiness without virtue. The stoics held that the only truly good thing about life is to pursue virtue; which is, living in accordance with nature. How are you living your life? Are you wittingly or unwittingly pursuing vice and expecting happiness? The stoics associated the pursuit of virtue with happiness because they believed that nature is divine – so, living according to nature is living according to the divine. Commit to pursuing virtue more than you pursue other things.

You cannot do this without discipline. Discipline is the basic action, philosophy, and mindset that will keep you progressing toward what you pursue. It is what sustains the stoic philosophical system. We will discuss it in chapter 3. For now, let's recap what we have learnt:

- Stoicism is a philosophical system built on logic, physics, and ethics. Without any one, the system collapses.
- Logic is how we think of the world. Ethics is the practical way we live based on what's divine. Physics is the divine universe.
- Pursuing virtue will produce happiness.

3

MARCUS AURELIUS AND SELF-DISCIPLINE - DISCIPLINE IS FREEDOM

'You could be good today, but instead, you are choosing tomorrow.' – **Marcus Aurelius.**

We are living in a time when many people struggle with uncertainty, fear, and doubt. The constant question in everyone's mind is – how do I find the strength to keep going? How am I to interpret life? Do hard times make you better? Tough times can make you feel as if it is the end of the world even though life never really stops moving. So, what are you to do then? Can a crisis make you better? The stoics would give a resounding 'yes' to that question. A crisis can make you better if you have the right mindset. It can teach you to let the past go, trust your gut, become stronger, forgive, and other lessons. But why do most people go through crises and never learn?

It turns out that no personal achievement, goal, or success can be achieved without self-discipline and many people lack that. They begin whatever endeavor without the determination to see it to the end. Inevitably, when a crisis hits, they move to the next thing, only to repeat the cycle. Self-discipline is the most important attribute you need to achieve any type of excellence. Like we said in the previous chapter, it is what you need to keep going toward your pursuit of virtue. It is the most practical of all stoic philosophies. In this chapter, we will explore what discipline is, the things getting in the way of self-discipline, and how to cultivate it, as learnt from Marcus Aurelius.

WHAT IS SELF-DISCIPLINE?

By definition, self-discipline is the ability to keep going, push yourself, and stay on course regardless of what you are feeling. It is something most people want, but one that is getting more difficult to develop. No wonder people are concerned about creating constructive habits, as evidenced by the increasing number of months set aside for this – No Nut November, Stoptober, Dry-January, you name it! During these months, people gather and try to promote self-discipline and abstinence from habits like porn and drinking. These are great ideas as they point to a willingness to adopt positive habits. But, as most people inevitably find out, changing habits is not very easy.

How often have you made goals or created a plan, promised yourself that this time you will do things differently, only to give up after a few days? How many times have you bowed to your impulses and returned to your habits? Discipline is about overcoming your short-term desires. Whether your goal is to build your business, spend more time with your family, or lose some weight, you need discipline to get there. You need to overcome your impulses to snack, waste your time on movies, or whatever the temptation.

I am not saying that the temptation will not be there if you become disciplined. You will feel the desire to slack off, for example. Self-discipline is the ability to resist that feeling. The more you resist it, the more disciplined you become. This is because discipline is like a muscle. I have to mention here that discipline is not the same as motivation. Motivation can help you to do things, but it ebbs and flows. If you rely on motivation alone, you will procrastinate, or fall back into your old habits. Discipline is consistent. It helps you move even when you are unmotivated. Discipline is freedom.

WHY IS IT HARD TO BECOME DISCIPLINED?

Developing discipline is not easy. It is like going uphill, hiking a mountain without a summit. Two things make it even harder to develop discipline:

Temptation

We are surrounded by so many distractions and sources of temptations that it is harder to resist our impulses. I am thinking of things like YouTube, video games, and social media, most of which are designed to compete for our attention and keep us hooked. All this noise makes it harder to achieve self-discipline, but it should be no excuse.

Zero resistance

The easier your life is, the less the opportunities there are to be disciplined. Ease causes discipline to atrophy and today's world is all about ease. Just look around – Amazon gives you convenient next day delivery, you can order food and have it in 30 minutes, social media gives you dopamine hits whenever you want them, with Netflix, you can watch anything you want, whenever. The list goes on. Instant gratification is eliminating opportunities to be self-disciplined. It is making us impatient people with low attention span.

Unfortunately, as the retail and business world move toward offering us convenience, it is also removing our sources of resistance. Resistance is needed for discipline to grow. Too much comfort is a trap. Excess comfort may be getting in the way of your self-discipline. You need resistance. It is what catalyzes growth. It shows you your limits and abilities and allows you to grow beyond them. So, what then are we to do? How do you grow self-discipline?

BUILDING SELF-DISCIPLINE WITH MARCUS AURELIUS

Most of the time, our ego will want us to run away from any sort of discomfort or resistance. This always happens at the beginning of any new pursuit. It is reasonable to expect it as you start implementing stoic wisdom. Fortunately, the stoics didn't keep silent about this matter. Marcus Aurelius arguably has the most to say about self-discipline, which is the essence of stoicism. He held one of the most influential positions in the world during his time. If he wanted, he could have had anything he desired. During his rule, he found time to write *'Meditations'* which is where you'll find the following insights about building self-discipline.

Find your purpose

Marcus Aurelius believed that everyone has a purpose – a thing we were created to do. He taught that it is our moral duty to find and achieve that purpose. It is purpose that will empower you to wake up every morning and do what you must do. If you clearly understand what your goals are and how everything you have to do contributes to those goals, then you are more likely to complete every daily task. The most significant source of self-discipline is to know your why. Once you know your why, even if you do not know what to do, you only need to start. If you want to become an author, just write something every day. Do it because you are meant to do it. Your purpose gives you an internal drive that moves you forward. Self-discipline is about finding that compelling reason to keep doing something.

Trust in yourself

Marcus Aurelius once wrote, 'make your desire a rock. Quench your appetites and keep your mind centered on you.' After you identify your purpose, your next task is to come up with a practical action plan to reach your goal. Do not just commit to the overarching goal; also commit to the little actions that will move you forward. Commit to doing whatever it takes regardless of the challenges. Self-discipline keeps you on course regardless of your emotional, mental, or physical state. Everything you want out of life – the things you want to be, do, or have, depend on your ability to do what you must to achieve your goal whether or not you are motivated to do it.

THE POWER OF STOICISM

As you create your action plan, make sure you build it on small milestones that you can accomplish every day. This gives you a sense of control over what you are doing. It helps you to avoid feeling overwhelmed. Being overwhelmed can cause you to procrastinate, which eventually causes you to digress or stagnate. When that happens, you cannot possibly say you are self-disciplined.

Be there, everyday

According to Marcus Aurelius, every life is built by different life actions. You have to be satisfied whenever one daily action achieves the best goal it could, that day. It is like this; after you find your purpose and form a good plan, you can still fail to be disciplined. You can fail to be consistent. Being there every day is about consistency. Show up and put in the work. The more you show up, the easier it will be to show up the next time. Self-discipline is the habit of consistency. Every day when you wake up, remind yourself that the day is new and it makes a new life. Focus on what is before you.

Voluntarily expose yourself to hardship

In one of his journal entries, Marcus Aurelius wrote, 'we should practice discipline in the small matters and then move on to bigger things.' In today's world where convenience is king, it will be more helpful to heed his advice and expose yourself to hardship, voluntarily. Voluntary hardship is about constantly testing yourself and making your life a bit uncomfortable as part of your routine. That way, you harden yourself for the day when you need to be truly tough. Voluntary hardship could be anything, from taking cold showers to not smoking. As you expose yourself to these hardships, you will start to see that you can live without some of these comforts.

Do not victimize yourself

Marcus was a big advocate of doing what you need to do without whining. Statements like 'I was born like this,' or 'I was never taught anything else,' make you a victim. They are excuses that help you justify staying as you are instead of doing better. They stem from a 'why me?' victim mentality, which absolves you of responsibility and works against self-discipline. Train yourself to frame things to empower yourself rather than pity yourself. Do not pawn off the blame when things go wrong. Self-discipline demands that you be a person of action; who does not relinquish their control and shirk responsibility.

Delay gratification

Marcus Aurelius taught that human beings are meant to do their part to put things into order, the same way birds, ants, and bees do. According to the stoics, people were not just born to feel nice. It is noble to do what nature demands and you cannot do that without delayed gratification. Delayed gratification is about waiting to get what you desire. It is resisting temptation as you stick to your goals – you put off what you want in the moment so that you can get something better in the future.

Ignore the critics

'Don't give small things more time than they deserve.' This is what Marcus Aurelius had to say about naysayers. When other people blame you, hate you, or criticize you, it is more about who they are. When you accept this truth, then you realize that you do not need to get anxious about others' opinions of you. It is bound to happen if you start pursuing your purpose and doing whatever it takes to achieve it. Naysayers typically criticize out of fear or shame over their own perceived lack of self-discipline. Engaging with them is a waste of energy. Do not give them your time. Instead, use feedback from people you respect and ignore all other voices.

Review your days

The rational soul is self-aware. It flourishes under self-examination and thrives with self-determination. It succeeds in the pursuit of its purpose. One of the most significant ways to become self-disciplined, according to Marcus Aurelius, is to study yourself and know your blind spots. Be honest and brutal as you do this. Make a habit of introspecting every evening as you actively gather information about who you are. Then, formulate answers to your weak spots. Ask yourself every day, 'what went well?' 'Where was my discipline tested?' 'What can I do better?' Then, after answering these questions, do not beat yourself up. Forgive yourself and resolve to do better tomorrow.

How self-disciplined are you?

THE POWER OF STOICISM

Marcus Aurelius thought of stoicism, not as a grand and judging instructor, but as a soothing balm to an injury. Epictetus rightly described life as brutal, narrow, punishing, and confining. Stoicism gives us the help we need to make the best of such a life. In this chapter we have established that:

- Self-discipline is about mastering our impulses.
- It can be built like a muscle, when there is resistance.
- Marcus Aurelius provided a map to growing self-discipline which includes things like delayed gratification, ignoring naysayers, and showing up every day.

In the next chapter, we ask ourselves, how do we apply stoicism to our lives to make them flourish? We will look at Epictetus' metaphors for life and glean from their wisdom to learn how to live a happy and virtuous life.

4

EPICTETUS' DETAILED INSTRUCTION FOR LIFE – ATTITUDE MATTERS

'How long will you wait before you demand the best for yourself?'
– Epictetus.

I t has been often said that our attitude in life matters. It is our attitude that influences how we act. If we have the right attitude, we get good results. All the hand-shakes and smiles in the world will not get you far if you have the wrong attitude. But little has been said about what that right attitude is, and even less about how to get it. What is the best life you can live and how do you cope with whatever life throws at you? How do you flourish? The stoic attitude is the answer. It is about understanding that the things others do are neither your responsibility nor your problem. Everyone of us bears responsibility for our daily thoughts and actions.

EPICTETUS' METAPHORS FOR LIFE

Epictetus employed some metaphors for life to explain that attitude. Here, we will explore Epictetus' metaphors to help you unpack the stoic attitude for life and adopt it as your own.

Life is a festival

Epictetus saw life as a festival that has been arranged for us by God. When you see life this way, you see it as something to enjoy. You are able to deal with any hardships that come your way because you have your eye firmly focused on the larger picture. You are aware of the grand play that you are part of. As part of the players in the festival, Epictetus asks you to find out what your purpose is. Was it not God – the festival planner – who brought you here? What was his reason? Did he not make you a mortal? Epictetus believed that your mortality, the little portion of flesh that you are on this earth, is meant to be enjoyed. You can participate with God for a short time in his festival and his pageant, so why don't you go ahead and enjoy it? The whole idea of stoic ethics is to enjoy your part in the festival, while contributing by living and fulfilling your duty as a good citizen of God's great city.

Life is a game

In *Discourses of Epictetus*, as Epictetus encouraged his students to embrace and accept the fact that some external things have no moral charge, he wrote that we should be like dice players. In a game involving dice, neither the counter nor the dice have any real value. The thing that matters and that can be either good or bad, is how you play the game. The stoic attitude looks at life that way. In another example, Epictetus talks about the experience of playing a ball game. In that moment, when the players are running and fighting for the ball, no one thinks of the ball as a bad or good thing. The only important thing is whether the players can catch or throw the ball with the required skill. What matters is the dexterity of the players, their good judgment, and their speed. A player has played well if they deployed their skill and faculties effectively.

In other parts of his writing, Epictetus uses the gaming metaphor when talking about suicide. A player stops playing the game when they are no longer enjoying it. That is the way it should be in life, according to him. No, he was not advocating for suicide, but arguing that people stop living when life becomes unbearable. His point: when you see life as a game, then the call is for you to get into the ring and play. You cannot afford to stand on the sidelines and offer critique as if you will get an opportunity to replace a player. The onus is for you to take your position and throw the ball.

Life is like weaving

Epictetus connected this metaphor with the metaphor of life as a game. When weaving, the weaver uses wool to make cloth. The wool plays the same role the ball plays in the game metaphor. It is our duty to use the wool the way it is supposed to be used, and to make the best cloth that we can.

Life is a play

We discussed in a previous chapter how finding our purpose helps us build self-discipline. It helps us to remember who we are and why we are here. This metaphor deals with the 'here' in that statement. It regards life as a play, but also introduces the notion of accepting one's fate, whatever that fate is. We do not get to choose the role we play in the theater of life. We aim to play a certain role, but we must see that our attaining that role is a thing of fate. When you think of life like this, you always remember that you are an actor in a play, not the author. God will determine how that play pans out, whether it will be short or long. If he wants you to play the cripple, then that is what you will be. If he wants you to play the poor man, private person, or public official, see that you play your part well. It is your job to act well in the role given to you.

Life is an athletic contest

In this metaphor, you can see a connection between your training in the ethics of the stoics as preparation for flourishing in life, and someone's athletic training as preparation for getting into the arena to compete. Here, Epictetus was talking to people who are distressed because they do not have enough time to study as much as they would like to, or prepare for as they wish they could. If studying, then you are to think of it as a preparation for living – and living is made up of other things besides books. Imagine an athlete getting into a field to play. He walks to the center of the stadium and then breaks down into tears. When asked, he says that he is weeping because he is not outside exercising, but inside the stadium. Do you see how absurd that is? Yet how many times do you refrain from doing things because you do not have enough training?

What the fictional crying athlete forgets is that they were exercising for the stadium. The weight pumping and rock-climbing leads to that moment. Are you trying to pump weights when it is already time for action? It is like being on the precipice of a choice and then instead of making it, you ask for a treatise on the choice, to read. Reading this book and doing other exercises that prepare you to strive for the stoic ideal is a lot like athletic training. The training is sometimes unpleasant, difficult, and demanding, but it prepares you for the arena of life. When you think of life as a contest, you must think about making progress. When you are confronted with difficulty, remember that the contest is now – the Olympic games are happening. You can no longer delay the match.

Life is military service

The stoics believed that God governs the universe. They believed that whether or not you like it, everyone serves God. In this metaphor, Epictetus was teaching his students that they should live life trying to discharge their military service to the highest possible standards. If you are upset by all the things that you are obliged to do, this metaphor is for you. It reminds you that you should go through life as a soldier called to service. While there, one man has to stand guard, another one has to take the field, and a third has to reconnoiter. All of them cannot remain in the camp. No one would be served if they did.

The lesson here is that you do not neglect to fulfill your orders. You cannot go back to the general to complain. It is a pitiful thing to be a soldier in service and to keep whining instead of carrying out your duties. If everyone did that, no one would do anything – no soldier would raise a palisade, dig the trenches, or fight in the field. That is also true of the world. Every one of our lives is a campaign. It is for you to be the best soldier you can be, at the general's bidding. It is for you to divine the wishes of the general whenever you can and then execute them.

How do you see your life?

What attitude are you carrying with you through life? Are you failing to enjoy life, do your part, or throw the ball? In this chapter, we have seen that:

- Life is a festival, enjoy it.
- Life is a game. It is weaving, use your tools well.
- Life is a play, act your part well.
- Life is an athletic contest. Participate.
- Life is military service, discharge your responsibilities.

In the next chapter, we will explore what the stoics believed about virtue. Since there is no happiness without pursuing virtue, how do you pursue virtue and what do we mean by virtue?

5

STOIC VIRTUE EXPLAINED - THE HIGHEST GOOD

'If it is not right, do not do it. If it is not true, do not say it.'
– Marcus Aurelius.

The expression 'the highest good' was coined by Cicero, arguably Rome's greatest orator. The highest good refers to the thing that we should be aiming for in life. As I mentioned earlier, for the stoics, virtue is the highest good. The stoics said that whatever we face in life, no matter the shape it takes, is an opportunity for a virtuous response. Even scary and painful situations demand that you respond with virtue. They went on to say that happiness, reputation, success, love, and honor, all follow if you act virtuously. That way, the man with virtue has everything they need to live well. But what did the stoics mean by virtue? In this chapter, we will expand on their meaning of virtue and apply it to our lives. The stoics believed that there are four virtues – wisdom, temperance, courage, and justice.

UNDERSTANDING STOIC VIRTUE

Wisdom

According to Epictetus, the main goal of life is to know and separate issues so that you can see yourself clearly and know what you can and cannot control. He went on to add that good and evil are not in the uncontrollable external, but within. Good and evil are the choices we make. To know this is to know wisdom and virtue. Diogenes said that the stoics considered wisdom to be the ability to define what is good and evil and what is neither evil nor good. It is knowing what you should choose, what to fear, and what to be indifferent to. Once you have this knowledge, how you act changes.

As Viktor Frankl is credited with saying, between response and stimulus, there is a space where the power to choose lies. Within that space, wisdom has an opportunity to shine. The first step to growing in wisdom is recognizing that space. It is where you take the lessons you have read about and apply them to life or disregard them and then act irrationally and impulsively. As Seneca explained it, wisdom is the ability to harness philosophy and use it in life.

Temperance

In *Meditations*, Marcus Aurelius talked about tranquility, arguing that if you want to be at peace in life, do less, or do what is necessary. To live at peace is to do only what you need as a social being when the need arises. It is to remove what is non-essential. He advised his students to ask themselves in every situation: 'is this necessary?' Aristotle talked about the same idea but he called it the 'golden mean.' He went on to add that you find virtue in the space between deficiency and excess. Excess symbolizes dissatisfaction and discontentment. To live in excess is to cave to a self-defeating impulse.

In his writings, Epictetus said, 'restrain your desire – do not let your heart follow many things and you will have what you need.' Seneca had similar thoughts. He talked about limiting your wealth only to what is necessary and what is enough. Temperance is knowing that you have plenty when you have what you need. The stoics often talked of this type of self-control toward pleasure, triumph, material goods, and even admiration and pain. Temperance is about guarding against the extremes so that you do not rely on pleasure for your happiness or allow the inconstancy of pain to destroy your happiness.

Courage

If life is military service, as Epictetus taught, then you have to do your part to keep things moving. You have to realize that you are in a battle – a varied and long battle. Your station is key to winning the battle and you stay there for life. When Epictetus was probed about this view, he said that for people to thrive, they must be willing to resist and persist. Courage has been a timeless symbol of stoic philosophy. It is embodied by a lone knight in a war that he could not possibly win, but he keeps fighting nonetheless. Courage is Publius Clodius challenging Nero in a challenge that would cost him his life. It is Marcus Aurelius resisting the corruption of power and deciding to be good even though Rome was declining.

Courage is shown by the great southern stoics, choosing bravery, generation after generation. It is LeRoy choosing to fight the Klan. It is William Alexander adopting his cousins and Walker Percy resisting the racism common in his time and deciding to be a beacon of goodness. It is Publius Rufus facing his accusers and inspiring change. It is Seneca's dying words, 'he may kill me, but he does me no harm.' Each one of these fights, even though in some ways futile, demanded a lot of courage. They demanded a determination to resist the status quo.

Publius Clodius stuck his neck out when he talked openly about Nero. He lost because of it. The Percys risked status and safety when they stood up for the rights of others. Marcus Aurelius risked losing his power. That is courage to the stoics. It is the bravery to look misfortune in the face and risk all for a fellow man. It is the determination to stick to your principles even when it is inconvenient. It is speaking your mind and living by what you know to be true.

Justice

Marcus Aurelius taught that we are born to commit to justice in everything we do. Every just act is for the common good. Of the four virtues of stoicism, Marcus Aurelius thought justice to be the most significant. To him, justice births the other virtues – how impressive is selfish courage? Or of what good is wisdom employed for self-interest only? To understand justice as virtue, we have to consider Cicero, who had similar thoughts with Marcus Aurelius. He described justice as the crown of all other virtues. More than talking about 'the highest good,' Cicero lived by those words. Even though he was a senator in Rome, entering an important office at a very young age, Cicero did not just think of justice in the legal sense as we do today.

For men like Cicero and the stoics, justice was broad. It covers our duty to, and interactions with other people. It is the principle that governs the bond of society and maintains a community. It maintains that no one has a right to harm someone else, no one has a right to another's private property while common property is common, and we are born for others. It also includes the idea that people exist to do good to each other, guided by nature. It embodies steadfastness, truth, and good faith. To act unjustly is to do anything that harms another person.

The virtue of justice is probably the most radical of all stoic thought. It is the foundation for the belief that everything in the world is interconnected. We are all one, and as Marcus Aurelius put it, 'what injures the hive, injures the bee.' If you hurt others, you are hurting yourself because we are all connected. Epictetus expounded on the idea saying that expecting the best of ourselves is actively caring for other people. If that is true, and it is, then honoring equality and doing what is good for humanity is the most honorable thing a man can do.

How are you living your life?

If you want to live a free and happy life, you need virtue. Thankfully, virtue is not vague or grandiose. The stoics were not fond of complex ideas that could not be applied simply. In fact, if I had to describe virtue as the stoics saw it in one sentence, it would be this: a stoic holds that they can only control their response to the world and their response should be done with courage, justice, wisdom, and temperance. Life is not predictable. There are a lot of things you cannot control. That thought could leave you overwhelmed and crippled, or it could be freeing. In this chapter we have established that:

- Virtue is what ensures that the knowledge of things you cannot control is freeing.
- If you are virtuous, you know that regardless of what happens, you can use reason and make a choice. You know that you will try to do what is right, guided by virtue.
- Virtue is the only thing you can control – then, you let everything else fall into place.

How are you living your life? Are you responding to challenges with temperance, wisdom, courage, and justice? In the next chapter, we will talk about another stoic, Seneca, and what he taught about redeeming the time you have in this play called life.

6

SENECA AND MANAGING YOUR TIME

'Nothing wastes our life more than putting things off – it snatches away each day as it comes and robs us of the present by promising the future.' – **Lucius Annaeus Seneca.**

We have all had to deal with the challenges of managing time at work. You wake up feeling optimistic and excited – you are going to meet all your deadlines and then have enough time left to get a workout in and make a healthy meal. Then, life happens. You leave your house late and find traffic that makes things worse. You get to the office frustrated and a bit disoriented. Eventually, you settle down to do that job you have been procrastinating for a while, only to realize that you have meetings for the better part of the morning – and of course, you are already late for the morning meeting.

When you finally leave the last meeting of the day, you begin sorting out your emails. As you do that, you are called for a short meeting with your boss. He has an urgent request that will only take you 30 minutes. It ends up taking two hours. The day goes on like that until you return home, not having accomplished any one of the things you set out to do. What then? The good news is that you can reclaim your elusive hours by managing your time better. You can learn to manage your time rather than letting it manage you, with old wisdom from Lucius Annaeus Seneca.

Commonly called Seneca, Lucius was a statesman and a Roman stoic philosopher who rose to become one of the most powerful figures in the Roman empire. True to the nature of human life, his life had ups and downs. The man lived through sorrow, pain, controversy, and drama. When Nero became the emperor of Rome in AD 54, Seneca was made his close advisor. His life was going very well at the time. A few years later, their close relationship suffered. As a result,

Seneca was ordered by the emperor to commit suicide because he allegedly took part in a failed assassination attempt on Nero. It is likely that he was innocent. Yet, even when under the threat of death, he clung to his stoic beliefs. History says that he remained very calm when the suicide protocol was initiated.

Ancient Roman suicide protocol required that the veins are severed so that you can bleed to death. You also had to take poison. Seneca went through that. More than 2000 years later, we still talk about him and his writings are still highly influential. He talked about many areas of life including relationships, death, wealth, and happiness, but in this section, we will talk about his thoughts on making the most out of time.

Examine how you spend your days

It is not uncommon to hear people talk about how short time is. Seneca's thoughts went against this idea. He argued that you have all the time you need to live an extraordinary life provided you treat your time like it is your most precious resource. Most of the time, people are frugal with their money and property, but they squander their time as if it is of no value. Remember that you can regain money but you can never regain time wasted.

Seneca once said that time is only short if you waste it. Even though he acknowledged how finite time is, he argued that our wastefulness makes it even shorter. According to him, it is not that our lives are short, but that we waste them. We have a long enough life and generous enough time to go for our highest aims if we invest our time well. Seneca went on to say that life is long if you know how to use it. So how do you use your time?

If you are going to manage your time better, you have to start by figuring out how you spend it. You can try logging your days for a week to track what you do every day. Such an audit will help you know what is realistic to aim for in a day, where you waste time, and where you should focus your energies. As you do this audit, you will start to see how much time you spend on unproductive conversations, thoughts, and activities. You will get a clearer sense of how much time you need for some tasks. You will also be able to know when you are most productive during the day.

Make a schedule and integrate rewards

One of the mistakes people make when they are trying to manage their time better is going about their days without a plan. You need a schedule for every day before you begin it. Make it your habit to create a to-do list in the morning. Alternatively, at the beginning of each week, make a list of all the things that you have to accomplish and assign each to its own day. As long as your plans are on paper, you won't need to get anxious at night worrying about all the things you have not done. Besides, when you pre-plan, your subconscious will start processing your plans while you are asleep so you can wake up in the morning with fresh insights. Creating a clear plan will save you the time you lose jumping between tasks because you had no plan.

I am not saying that this will be simple, and neither did the stoics. Seneca added to this idea another step that can make it easier for you to stick to your plan – create an immediate reward for your goals. Research has proven that one of the reasons we procrastinate is the lasting tension between short-term reward and long-term goals, an idea called 'present bias.' According to Seneca, this bias is the greatest obstacle to living. Your brain imagines different versions of yourself – your future and your present self. Every time you create a goal for a better future, you plan for your future self who loves long-term rewards and discipline. When you have to act though, your present self fights your future self and wins most of the time.

You can deal with this problem Seneca's way – make the rewards for your goals immediate. For example, if you want to become a person who exercises regularly but you enjoy socializing, sign up to a gym or team sports. You will get to socialize as you work toward your goal. Get creative with your rewards and it will be easier to do everything you need to do every day.

Limit your tasks

A significant part of your schedule should be setting limits on how long some tasks should take rather than doing them until you finish; otherwise, it might feel like you are not making any progress. You can try taking a break after every hour to balance focus with rest so that you reduce mental strain and stay motivated. Once you finish the set time for a task, go to the next important thing. You will notice your productivity increasing as your to-do list grows shorter. However, do not be overambitious.

According to Seneca, if you obsessively pursue achievement and goals, you will become miserable and shorten the length of your life. Living that way will get you what you want, but you will have gotten it anxiously. If you make your life all about achievement, you have forgotten that time never returns. You hit a goal, and immediately, a new one takes its place. Ambition births ambition – you work for the sake of work, until there is no end to your misery. In case you are thinking that Seneca took it too far, consider today's consumerist culture. We strive to work longer and harder to get more things. The result? Burnout, unhappiness, anxiety, and stress. Limiting your tasks will remind you of your why and keep you from falling victim to the trap of consumerism.

Meditate on death

Seneca thought part of the reason we waste so much of the time we have is that we forget that no one comes out of life alive. We waste time because we live as if we have forever. We never think about how frail we are and how much time has already passed. We waste time because we imagine we have an abundant supply of it, even though the day we spend on some unimportant thing may be the last we have. By Seneca's wisdom, how we think about death affects the way we live. If we think death is far from us, we will take our days for granted and waste time. How often do you think about death? Has the inevitability and reality of it firmly settled in your heart?

Meditating about death will also help you to avoid wasting your time on vain planning. Most of the time, according to Seneca, we waste our days planning for the future, rather than living today. He went on to say that everyone lives their lives troubled by the future and weary of the present. He neither longs for or fears the next day, he who plans his today as if it were his last day. Thinking about death will help you stop postponing your happiness because you will see that the future you obsess about does not exist.

Do one thing at a time

One of the simplest ways to improve your time management skills is avoiding the need to multitask. Focus on one task at a time and do away with distractions. It will be tempting to multitask but if you cave, you are setting yourself up for failure. You will end up losing time and becoming less productive as you try to juggle different tasks. As a rule of thumb, avoid the trap of busyness. It is the ultimate distraction. Popular opinion exalts staying busy. It heralds busyness as though it were a virtue. Seneca thought of busyness as an illusion that actually steals your time. No one can pursue anything successfully if they are preoccupied.

Oftentimes, we blame social media, emails, and other people for our difficulties staying focused while the reality of it is that our internal state most influences our productivity. Busyness points to a negative internal state. It is simply a symptom. It is the avoidance of solitude and an escape from what is real. You cannot be very productive if you cannot sit quietly in a room, alone.

How are you spending your days?

Let's recap what we have learned in this chapter:

- Time is your most valuable, non-renewable resource. Treat it that way.

- Think about death and live like you are on borrowed time.
- Busyness is an illusion and multi-tasking is a lie.
- Make a schedule and reward yourself for tasks accomplished.

After auditing your days, how are you living each day? In a world of constant busyness, leave the hamster wheel of life and relish each day. It might be your last.

PART II

MASTER YOUR EMOTIONS LIKE A STOIC

7

5 THINGS THAT DISTURB INNER PEACE

'What upsets people is not things themselves, but their judgments about these things.' – **Epictetus.**

I n the previous chapter, I mentioned that you cannot be productive if you cannot sit by yourself in a room, quietly. Most people don't know what clarity of thought feels like. They are so used to a tumultuous inner world that inner peace sounds like a myth. The stoics were big on inner peace. In this section of the book, we will talk about dealing with negative emotions the stoic way so that you can experience some of that internal quietness. I will deal with each troublesome emotion in a chapter of its own, but first, let's explore the things that stand in the way of achieving inner peace. That way, you will know what you will be working to eliminate.

The desire to be validated

One of the things we cannot control is what others think of us. We can influence their opinion of us, but even if we did everything right, it is still up to them to validate us or not. There will be people who dislike you for no reason. That is the nature of life. Yet, the desire to be validated still steals peace from many people. To deal with this, you have to accept that it is weak to pursue other people's validation because that is not something you can pursue. Like Epictetus said, it is not virtue to pursue what is outside your control. You do not need to give up control of your happiness to others.

Anxiety over the past and worry about the future

Your mind will never be peaceful if you cannot let the past rest. If you carry with you events from the past, you burden yourself and your luggage keeps growing by the day. The problem is – you have no power to change the past. Besides, you cannot trust your mind to accurately retell

THE POWER OF STOICISM

the story of the past. Our minds retell those stories, clouded by bias. Instead, you need to learn the valuable lesson your past offers and let the event go while holding on to the lesson. Remind yourself of the transient nature of things. Marcus Aurelius said that time is like a river – as soon as something happens, it is carried away and another one takes its place.

Dealing with anxiety about the past is choosing to flow along the river of time without clinging to the past or expecting the future to be a certain way. Worry about the future is another common inner peace thief. How peaceful can you be if your mind is stuck in a future that is yet to happen? What use is there in dwelling on the countless 'what ifs?' There is a certain uncertainty to the future. It can bring anxiety if you do not accept it and always embrace whatever outcomes you get.

The attachment to perfection

Perfectionists bring themselves anxiety by desiring an ideal that can never be attained. They become restless because what they do is not good enough. As a result, no single result satisfies them. They live in a constant state of dissatisfaction with who they are and what they are capable of doing. Rather than pursuing perfection, pursue excellence. Excellence is achievable, but perfection isn't.

The fear of death

The other group of people are those who are afraid of death and are obsessed with stalling the process of aging. History has shown that aging and death are inevitable. True, you can extend your lifespan by embracing healthy habits and caring for your body, but in the long run, aging is inevitable. You cause yourself undue anxiety by failing to accept the inevitability of death.

The fear of the unknown

Another group, still, fears what they do not know. They fear flying when they have never been on a plane, or people from another culture because they are unfamiliar. It is natural to be alert around what is new, but fear of the unknown goes beyond the natural. It causes you to make up situations in your mind – fantasies about what could be – which steal your peace, and your trust in the process of being.

~

What things disturb your inner peace?

Whatever it is that disturbs your inner peace, does so by creating a narrative within that either causes anxiety, frustration, anger, or stress. It paints reality a different shade and causes you to act irrationally. You end up spending energy and time on things that you cannot change. The stoics had a way to deal with these big emotions, but before looking at those, let's recap what we have learnt:

- The fear of the future, of death, the desire to be validated, and other factors steal our inner peace when we let them.
- Anything that disturbs our inner peace does so by tapping into our inability to control our internal narrative and manage our emotions well.

We cannot control the world. There is no guarantee that the things we fear will not happen, but you can guarantee yourself that you will respond with a rational mind and empowered action by embracing the wisdom of the stoics.

8

HOW EPICTETUS
KEEPS CALM

'It's not what happens to you, but how you react to it that matters.'
– Epictetus.

We meet frustrations every day. We are bound to. Often, things do not go the way we hope. We encounter bad news. We get upset when fate seems to have a will different from ours. We try harder to control things and when it doesn't work, our expectation that things will work diminishes. Then, we find ourselves back at the start of the cycle dealing with similar frustrations. How do we get out of the loop? How do we stay calm in the thick of things to make a better decision?

Revise your understanding of the 'self'

Epictetus understood the 'self' in a narrower yet concentrated way than most people do. Most of us think of our reputation and status as part of our 'self.' We even feel the same way about our property. After all, those things are ours by law. Yet, it is this view that makes us feel disempowered or lacking control over what is 'us.' Epictetus' view was completely radical. He was at the mercy of his master, and never had much property, but his sense of self remained untouched. He once told his students: 'You can put my leg in chains but even Zeus himself could not overcome my will.' On a number of occasions, he even separated his will from his body. As a slave, his body belonged to his master.

We can learn from his attitude. In the end, our bodies are not ours even though we are free. If they were, then we could will away cancer or any other sickness. Things outside our control may impinge some of our freedoms, but never the freedom of our will. Our will will never be harmed if we grasp the fact that it is fully ours. If you grasp this lesson, then you will never give your peace of mind to anything or anyone but yourself.

Rehearse your intentions

Epictetus advises that if you want to remain calm when it matters, rehearse your intentions. Whenever you do something with a lot of factors out of your control, set a parallel intention to remain in line with nature. Decide beforehand that whatever happens, you will be rational. The stoics believed that people are 'possessed of reason.' Otherwise put, only human beings have the ability to reason. Acting in line with nature is acting with reason.

Epictetus gave his students an example of what it looks like to rehearse your intentions. At the time, it was an important leisure ritual to go to the public baths. Whenever he planned a visit, he would decide beforehand that if his possessions got stolen, he would keep his composure. Keeping his composure was the intention he set. Are you setting your intention? Imagine visiting a restaurant and finding that the table you pick has not been cleaned. What would you do? Would you still have a good time? Suppose you ask the waiter to clean the table and he ignores you. What then? Would you make a scene? The idea of setting your intention is realizing that it is entirely your choice to exercise reason.

Pause and study the situation

Epictetus dealt with difficulties by asking the question 'what is out of my control?' It is always shocking to understand how little control we have when we are riding an emotional wave. Train yourself to pause and ponder this question. It will strip away everything that is not yours to solve and leave you with a clear view of what is within your 'will.' When you understand what little you can control, you can comfort yourself knowing that only your impressions of the world are yours to control.

Decide how to move forward

Taking a pause will allow you to gain perspective, but that perspective will be wasted if you still act based on your emotion. Once you have a firm grip on what you can control, decide how you will control it. Epictetus spent the most of his life in slavery. Back then, slaves were dehumanized and robbed of their dignity and identity. His very name means 'property,' and yet he managed to exert control over his destiny by deciding how to respond to what he could control.

Can you keep calm in the face of frustration?

As we go about our lives, we are baited by fate to succumb to sadness, frustration, or annoyances. In this chapter we have learned that:

- How we respond is within our control.
- We can set our intentions beforehand to make sure we remain calm.
- It always pays to take a pause while in the heat of the moment.

9

CONTROLLING YOUR ANGER LIKE SENECA

'We should not control anger, but destroy it completely. What control is there for something that is fundamentally wicked?' – **Seneca.**

Seneca proposed a number of ways to manage anger. He frequently described anger as temporary madness. According to him, even when anger is justified, we should never act on it because it always affects our sanity. Here are five ways that you can control your anger like Seneca:

Remember that anger is destructive

Seneca never saw any utility in anger. He thought that anyone who is completely aware of anger's faults and its ability to impede proper judgment, is able to avoid becoming angry. Recognizing anger's potential for destruction is an important step for handling it. On the other side of the spectrum are Aristotle's thoughts on anger. Aristotle thought that anger is not always bad. For example, if you get angry within the right context and at the right time, your anger is justifiable. Those who agree with Aristotle believe that the trick lies in staying in the middle ground. To them, good temper is a virtue.

There was no good degree of anger with Seneca. This is not to say that he (and other stoics) was passive to injustice. The stoics believe in our ability to reason. They believed that reason should govern every sphere of life. Nothing could be more unreasonable than anger. From Seneca's perspective, anger is unnatural because it makes you a slave, it cannot be slowed down, and it is contagious.

Identify your triggers

If you think about it, some situations tend to make you angrier than other situations you encounter regularly. Find them. As Seneca puts it, your best bet is to deal with the sickness the moment you identify it, by keeping quiet and curbing the emotion. Being mindful of your triggers will help you know when you are about to get angry. Then, you can stop yourself effectively and in good time. If you are mindful, you will notice the patterns that make you angry and see the thoughts that trigger anger. Common triggers include:

- Getting mistreated by others
- Witnessing an injustice against yourself or someone you care about
- Rejection and other threats to self-esteem
- Prejudice and discrimination

A trigger could be any variation of the above. Once you identify your trigger you will be able to respond to it in good time. When you expect to be angry, then you can express your anger constructively.

Count to five before reacting

Here, the idea is not the number you are counting to, but the break before you respond. According to Seneca, you can cure anger by waiting out the initial passion. Once it dies down, it takes with it the fogginess it shrouds the mind with and you can see a bit clearer. The idea is to inhabit the space between the stimulus and your response. I must mention here that anger is not a good guide to your happiness. It makes you impetuous and rigid and gets in the way of problem solving. While fear may make you flee, anger makes you run toward confrontation.

It has been said that anger is often at the heart of retaliation and revenge. No wonder, as even the best intellectuals turn to expletives when they are angry. Every time you feel angry, remove yourself from the triggering situation and withhold action until you feel at peace before you respond. If you get an enraging email, sit with it and respond after a couple of days. If you are in a fight, walk away and if you can, get advice from someone else. In the heat of anger, you are likely to make choices you will regret.

Use art to calm yourself

Seneca thought that the hot-tempered should avoid demanding studies because their mind should not be occupied with hard tasks. He recommended pleasurable arts for them. If you struggle with anger, try reading poetry, listening to music or stories, and let your mind be calmed by the gentleness and refinement of art. Find art that soothes you and it will help your pursuit of a peaceful mind. Psychologists call this type of anger management *'expressive theory.'* Here, you are encouraged to scream, yell, or workout to get rid of pent-up anger.

In a counseling session, a therapist might help you to identify your unresolved anger issues. Then, they would recommend drama, art, or music therapy. The idea is that these will help your body heal from the unresolved anger. Soothing art will make you feel happy and energetic. It will also help to stabilize your mood.

Picture yourself as the one in the wrong

Seneca advised his students to put themselves in the shoes of the man making them angry. It is an inaccurate estimate of our worth that makes us angry, coupled with an unwillingness to accept the treatment we would dish to others. Putting yourself in the shoes of others is a good way to deal with anger. It will remind you of the times you have acted the same way. Always ask yourself these questions:

- Have I acted wrongly before? How many

times?
- Have I ever been violent?
- Have I ever been mean to someone and regretted it later?
- Have I ever manipulated someone?

The idea is to formulate the question to help you consider the situation from the other person's perspective.

How are you dealing with your anger?

We all get angry occasionally. The best you can do is:

- Recognize your triggers.
- Shift your perspective to the offenders.
- Rely on art to calm yourself.
- Take a break before responding.
- Meditate on the destructiveness of anger.

It is always better to heal than to take revenge. Vengeance will waste your time and energy and expose you to more injuries. As Seneca put it, anger will always outlast hurt.

AMOR FATI - DEALING WITH ANXIETY

'How does it help... to make troubles heavier by bemoaning them?' – **Seneca.**

Y ou can make yourself anxious by excessively worrying about the future. This anxiety can show up as short-term anxiety over a planned event or it could be long-term, over a future that is out of your control. To deal with anxiety, the stoics had a trick called 'Amor Fati' which will be the focus of this chapter. 'Amor Fati' means 'loving your fate.' There is strength in embracing whatever happens. Nietzsche, a German philosopher who rejected stoicism but loved the idea of Amor Fati, wrote that people want things to stay the same but the formula for greatness is to endure what is necessary and to love it.

The stoics embraced this attitude. Marcus Aurelius, in *Meditations*, wrote that 'a blazing fire makes brightness and flame of everything thrown in it.' Epictetus, a man who was crippled as a slave, echoed the thought, saying that instead of forcing things to work the way you want, or wishing for things to happen your way, wish that whatever happens, happens the way it does and then you will be happy. This is 'Amor Fati.' It is the mindset that you can make the best out of whatever happens. You treat every moment, regardless of its challenges, as something to embrace, not to avoid. You resolve to not only be okay with whatever happens, but to love it and let it make you better.

Amor Fati is the idea that for an infinite period of time, everything will recur to infinity. When Nietzsche coined the term, he meant to explain the desire to live the same life over and over for eternity. It is about accepting what happens so that whatever happens, the response is Amor Fati. If anxiety for the future is crippling you, then like the stoics, you can simply, 'love your fate.'

Remember that life goes on

Imagine that there are two versions of you – the stoic you and the anxious you. In the company you work, there are going to be layoffs. You heard the news by mistake when you walked past your boss' office as you were leaving early for a doctor's appointment. Your doctor told you that you may have cancer and your partner thinks it is your fault, so your relationship is not going so well. The obstacles in your life are so big that your life will change significantly. The change makes the anxious you very worried because your mind judges the possible change as either desirable or undesirable.

When the changes we encounter in life are desirable, we experience them as pleasure. When the situation is undesirable, we experience deep pain. Either way, life goes on. In your imagined situation, how much anxiety could you prevent by reminding yourself that life still goes on? No matter where you end up, you will still only have the present, never the past and never the future.

You only have the present

In the imaginary situation I just told you about, we could conclude that your life is changing in an undesirable direction. The 'anxious you' begins worrying and that worry keeps you up at night. You wonder whether you will be laid off. Will your partner leave you? What if cancer gets in the way of getting another job? Some of these questions are things you can change and others are not. In the end, your future is outside your grasp. And that is the source of the problem – you are trying to control the future because you cannot handle insecurity. But what if you only focused on what you can do in the present?

Embrace fate

The stoic way is to embrace fate regardless of what happens. Amor Fati is not about sitting all day and checking out of life. It is about making the best of every moment. It is working toward your goals and pouring your all into them, but when things don't work out, you accept your fate. If you end up keeping your job, great! If you are laid off, you do the best you can with it. If you have no cancer, great! If you do, then you make your life count in spite of it. If your partner stays, great! If they leave, good riddance! You can now focus on yourself and who knows, maybe you will meet someone else in the future.

Do you embrace your destiny?

Anxiety silently destroys life. It is an internal wrecking ball that can leave you incapacitated. But it does not have to steal your happiness. Amor Fati ensures that you cannot go wrong, and if you cannot go wrong, you do not have to worry. When you do not have to worry, anxiety does not have to sap your energy. Here, we have seen that you can deal with anxiety by:

- Reminding yourself that life goes on.
- Staying in the present.
- Embracing your fate, no matter what.

11

WHY WORRY ABOUT WHAT ISN'T REAL? - SENECA

'To be truly happy is to enjoy the present without anxiously depending on the future - not to amuse yourself with hopes and fears, but resting satisfied. The greatest blessings are within us and within our reach. He is wise who is content with his lot; who does not wish for what he does not have.' – **Seneca.**

Writing a letter to his friend, Seneca said that there are more things likely to frighten us than there are things to crush us – we suffer more because of our imagination than because of reality. This is true for the majority of worriers. They are more occupied with the future and with the possibilities than with the present. During the day, their

THE POWER OF STOICISM

thoughts stay on what's coming. At night, they lay awake planning and calculating their defense against some unwanted thing that may happen. Even though they try to control the future, they never leave the present because the future only exists in our minds. So how do you deal with worry, the stoic way?

Get a reality check

Worriers forget one thing – you cannot live in the future; you can only predict it. True, you can plan for some things that may happen, but the present does not always conform to our plans. Because the tendency of worry is to keep you fixed on the endless possibilities, when you catch yourself in that loop, give yourself a reality check. Remind yourself that you only have now and worry is a liar. The future is an illusion. Only the present is real.

Acknowledge all your groundless fears

Holding on to the idea that the future is an illusion is not about denying the passage of time. It is about acknowledging what is happening in the moment and its transience. We are constantly exposed to novelty the way a mountain top is exposed to blizzards. No one can control a blizzard any more than they can control the wind. It comes from whenever and decides its speeds and what it carries. The mountain cannot predict the blizzard and neither should it try. We are the same. We cannot predict circumstances. We can only endure.

So, when you are faced with groundless fears of the future, remind yourself that something is coming but you cannot know what or when it will hit. No matter how well you prepare or try to make it out, you will still be shooting in the dark. The future is only ideas that are yet to come to life. When those ideas grip you, face them and let them go. Separate the truth from speculation. As Seneca puts it, 'the truth has definite boundaries.' Illusions are uncertain and delivered through guesswork – they are born from a frightened mind.

Fortify your mind

Seneca noticed that some things affect us even before they appear and continue to oppress us even though they never appear. This is true when we get into the habit of imagining, anticipating, or exaggerating sorrow. The mind learns to create false shapes of darkness when no darkness

THE POWER OF STOICISM

can be found. It twists words to cast doubt, create grudges, and lengthen anger. This habit is not just unpleasant, but research shows that worry also makes you sick. This means that even though the future is not yet real, you worry yourself sick because of it.

The antidote to this is fortifying your mind with truth about reality and about the changing nature of fortune and misfortune. Seneca was not a man without difficulties in his life, but he was able to cope with all the misfortune that came his way. He stood his ground because he learned that misfortune and fortune cannot be predicted. Fortify your mind with this truth and watch out for the influences you allow into your mind. Not only are people ignorant of what will happen and how events will unfold, but also the nature of the events. This means that you should be careful when judging fate. Sometimes a misfortune you anticipate comes to fruition.

Remember that bad fortune is fickle

The final antidote that Seneca gave for worry regards the fickleness of fortune. A story is told of a Buddhist man chased by a tiger. As he sought refuge, he jumped into an old well. There was a snake at the bottom and so he held on tightly to a root that was poking out of the walls of the well. It turned out that the root was being eaten by mice. It seemed that his fate was sealed when suddenly, fortune gave him an out - the tiger that was leaning at the mouth of the well dropped, falling on the snake. The loosened root gave in and the man fell just in time to meet the tail of the snake that hit him up out of the well. The point? – hardship can befall anyone at any point, but it does not stay forever.

Observe with care

Dealing with worry does not mean closing your eyes to all the bad things that could happen. Seneca did not advocate for ignorance. Instead, he advises that you observe with care. On one end of the spectrum, it is unwise to deny misfortune. On the other end, the smallest sign of adversity should not usher you into panic mode. The key is to toe the line between obsession and ignorance. Mindfully assess your situations but keep your options open, remembering that not everything is as it seems.

How is worry affecting your life?

Our judgments about the present or future events are often wrong and our fears often have no basis. You can deal with worry by:

- Grounding yourself in reality.
- Teaching your mind to tell truth from illusion.
- Observing the future with care.
- Remembering the fickleness of fortune and misfortune.

12

MASTER SELF-CONTROL

'No evil propensity of the human heart is so powerful that it may not be subdued by discipline.' – **Seneca.**

The stoics talked about self-control a lot. Marcus Aurelius, for example, talked about setting limits to consumption and comfort. Epictetus talked about watching our language so that our talk does not become vulgar. Self-control helps you to stay away from acting on impulses and pursuing addictive behavior. It helps you to stay focused on what is important. When the stoics made a distinction between what you can and can't control, the idea is to focus on what you can control – yourself.

A self-controlled person is less likely to be enslaved to external approval from things or people. They will be less ruled by things that are not up to them. Temptations and triggers hold less sway over you when you are self-controlled, which strengthens your position in the world. Upon encouragement from a friend, I once went on a 72-hour food fast. I was not supposed to eat anything for three days. I struggled the most on day one but on the second day, I was able to work normally. This changed how I think about food. Before the fast, I thought that if I didn't eat for a day, I would faint. It turned out I was just fine. The lesson? – Many desires and needs we have do not come from the body, they come from ideas in our minds.

After the 72-hour abstinence from food, my relationship with it has never been the same. I became less needy, knowing that I will be able to function without food for a while. I no longer worry so much about food. That is what growing self-control does for you – it takes away unnecessary worry and anxiety and allows you to tell between real and imagined needs. So how do you develop self-control like the stoics?

Abstain from something you love for days

Seneca once reflected on festivities happening in Rome. There, the Romans indulged in every pleasure. He posited that it is a courageous thing not to take part in the festivities, and even more courageous to participate differently – without extravagance. His whole idea was to detach ourselves from luxury once in a while to test the mind. Seneca advises that if you want to build self-control, you should reserve some days where you live in the poorest possible way. You will demystify everything you feared about that condition. The thing you abstain from could be anything from social media and the internet to your smartphone use. Get creative and you will see your many options.

Limit your leisure time

Marcus Aurelius advised that you can develop self-control by limiting your leisure time. He taught that we are not meant to spend our days on leisure if we are to learn from other things on the planet. The bees never stop doing their job and neither do the spiders. Why should human beings be any different? Not all animals are the best ideal for hard work, but Marcus Aurelius was on to something – living as we should, that is, in moderation.

Wait a moment before you eat

Of all the ways put forward for developing self-control, this is probably the funniest, but one of the most difficult. Whenever you serve food, wait a moment in front of your plate. Do not start eating immediately. Then, when you do, chew a specific number of times before you swallow.

How intimate are you with hardship?

Self-control familiarizes us with hardship by exposing us to things other people go through regularly and makes us more content with the things we have. It makes us less dependent on what we imagine we need to make us happy. The idea of these exercises is to become 'intimate with poverty,' in the words of Seneca. That way, fortune will not catch you with your pants down. So, let's recap:

- Self-control keeps us from being enslaved to people and things.
- You can develop self control by attempting any type of fast, limiting your leisure time, and waiting a while before you eat.

13

BUILDING SELF CONFIDENCE WITH MARCUS AURELIUS

'You want the praise of people who kick themselves every fifteen minutes, the approval of people who despise themselves. Is it a sign of self-respect to regret nearly everything you do?'
– Marcus Aurelius.

The stoics believed that only what is done virtuously can make you truly happy. This means that you cannot be happy through external gains. Most of the time in our lives, we are required to be bold and to endure almost painful things to create the extraordinary. Very few things come easy. You have to do the work, be patient and strategic to reap any rewards in life. This takes courage. As it turns out, not everyone is willing to develop that courage. Yet, nothing is as satisfying as knowing that you are making a difference in the world.

Whether you are an entrepreneur or an employee, regardless of where you fall in society, life will demand that at some point, you take a bet on yourself or you lose. That is where self-confidence comes in. It will allow you to pursue your life's purpose even before you see the payoffs. Self-confidence is a form of practice. It is not an idea. It is not words of affirmation. It is not something you only know intellectually. Self-confidence stems from within. It is shaped by the things you do. The stoics recommend that you grow your self-confidence by:

Accepting who you are

Self-acceptance is inevitably tied to self-confidence. The stoics understood that whenever you run from your dark side, you also run from your light. Running from your dark side is running away from the things that would make you stand alone, calling the hero within to rise and pushing you to be a more virtuous person. Marcus Aurelius said that the greatest crime we can commit against ourselves is to disown our inadequacies. In doing so, we also disown our greatness. To grow your self-confidence, remind yourself that you are complete and whole as you are. No one expects you to be perfect and neither should you.

If you are overweight, for example, accept what is, then if you must, work to change it from a place of love, rather than self-policing. This idea applies to every shortcoming. But the idea is to love yourself even before you get to the solution. Nothing does more for your self-confidence than accepting the parts of yourself that you had disowned.

Fully own your life and your choices

A negative view of self inevitably disempowers. It causes you to delegate responsibility even for your actions and choices. Growing self-confidence is about taking responsibility for your choices, not as the recipient of moral blame, but as the underlying causal agent driving your behavior. Teach yourself that you can pursue the things you love and get to your goals because you control your life. Even if your actions sometimes get obstructed, no one can touch your intentions. All you need to do is follow Marcus Aurelius' advice – accommodate and adapt.

Stand up for what you believe

You cannot live authentically, and boldly, without standing up for what you believe. Standing up for what you believe grows your self-confidence. It enables you to live out your innermost feelings and convictions. It gives you the pen to write your own story. Our intuition has a way of letting us know when we fall out of alignment with our values – we often call this 'gut feeling.' We cannot explain it, but we know it is there. When you have a gut feeling, investigate it, and follow its dictates. It will grow your self-confidence. As a side note: if you do not stand up for what you believe, no one else will.

$\sim$

What are you doing to build your self-confidence?

From this chapter we have seen that:

- Self-confidence allows you to write your own story.
- You can grow your self-confidence by standing up for what you believe, owning your life and choices and accepting yourself.

PART III

THE POWER OF
INDIFFERENCE

14

HOW TO CARE LESS

'I am always amazed by this: we love ourselves more than we love others, but we are more concerned about their opinion than ours. If a god came to us – or even a wise person – and prohibited us from hiding our thoughts, or imagining anything without making it public, we would not last one day. That is how much we value other people's opinions rather than our own.'
– Marcus Aurelius

One American sociologist described our unproductive and irrational obsession with what others think like this: 'I am not the person I think I am and I am not who you think I am. I am who I think you think I am.' If you think that is strange, it is because it is. Some people are so obsessed about other people's opinions that they make life choices based on them. You end up putting undue importance on external validation, so much so that you cannot be happy in life. But what did the stoics have to say about this? How can stoic wisdom help you to care less?

Get inside the mind of the 'judger'

Suppose someone was judging you. Suppose it was all true – that whenever you make a life choice, this person sits astride their high horse and gasps at every move you make. Maybe they have better ideas about who you should be. Of course, that's ridiculous, but what if it were true? Marcus Aurelius recommends getting inside the mind of that 'judger.' When you get insults or flak from others, get inside their soul – see what kind of person they are. Then, you will find that you do not need to work so hard to impress them.

The point Marcus Aurelius was making was that most of the time, we blindly accept the things other people throw at us without examining why they have a right to throw those things. Would you take driving advice from someone you know is a bad driver? Would you agree to be guilted about your finances by someone who is deep in debt? Nor should you take to heart the words of people you do not admire. If you do not respect a person and their choices, you do not need to listen to them. If you want to stop caring about the opinions of others, take a minute and look at those people. You will find that you are doing just fine without breaking your back for their approval.

Consult with logic

When you look at approval-seeking logically, you see that there is no need to fear abandonment. In most cases, we are not even in danger when others disapprove of us or dislike us. True, it is preferable to be loved by those around us – it is preferable to get likes on Facebook, but you do not need them for survival, or to be happy. As the stoics saw it, a good reputation is a 'preferred in-different.' It is nice to be well thought of, but if you are not, you can still live a virtuous life. In other words, if you live well, why should it concern you what others think?

Marcus Aurelius, in his writing, displayed a lot of contempt for validation seeking, asking what the price is. 'What is an audience clapping more than people clacking their tongues?' He asked. As far as he was concerned, public praise is simply the sound of clacking tongues. Think about it – what is the nature of receiving likes on Facebook, for example? It is nothing more than screen pixels and bodily movements that give us a temporary feeling of pleasure. But true to the nature of any type of external validation, it never makes us content in the long-term. It only leaves us craving for more validation, and what good is a life lived chasing validation?

How do you approach the desire to seek approval?

The more we value things that we cannot control, the less control we have, and the opinion of others is not something we can control. So, instead of obsessing over what others think about you, you can simply care less by:

- Getting inside of the 'judger' to see that they have no right to judge you.
- Approaching the desire to seek approval with logic to see that what others think about you is none of your business.

15

BE A LOSER IF NEED BE

'Think of the things you do not have as non-existent. Focus on what you have and what you value most. Think about how much you would be missing if you did not have them, but do it cautiously. Do not be so satisfied that you begin to overvalue what you have – it should not upset you to lose them.' – **Marcus Aurelius**

Whether you just got a promotion or landed a new job making more money, for most people, this means spending more. Perhaps you get those shoes you always wanted. Maybe you sign up for a membership in a gym. After all, you earned it. Then, if you are not paying attention, you wake up one day and find that you have 50 pairs of shoes and 39 different ties. You have a nice car and a second nicer one. You have five different and equally necessary sets of earphones. You have fallen prey to lifestyle creep and the sad part of it is – you are never at peace with any of it because you no longer recognize what matters to you. Life could not be emptier.

Lifestyle creep happens when the more you earn, the more you spend. It looks different for different people. For some people, it is about an ever-growing taste for finer things. It could also be about paying higher rent, eating gourmet food, and attempting expensive hobbies. You get the idea. The problem is, lifestyle creep edges out your financial goals. Your new lifestyle takes priority over your financial wellbeing and soon enough, over your emotional wellbeing. Even though you are earning plenty, you may end up in debt or living paycheck to paycheck.

You realize you are heading in this direction when things you considered luxury have now become necessities, or when you spend on expensive haircuts and products without giving it much thought. The one-time expenses that used to sting become more comfortable. The worst part is, it starts to feel like you are making progress while in fact, you are hurting yourself. Epictetus' wisdom for life can help you to keep a check on yourself so that you are no longer controlled by things:

Be a loser

In today's world, the idea of a 'loser' is a shadow cast by stories of winners or people with fame, power, and money. But the stoics thought of success as broader than fame, power, and money. As far as Epictetus was concerned, being a loser was nothing to be ashamed of. Today, you are rejecting someone if you call them a loser. It is an insult based on sex, gender, disability, race, or whatever other divide. Ultimately, the loser loses status. But for the stoics, the word did not have that heap of contempt associated with it. The stoics were indifferent to fame, power, and money. You can be too.

The idea is to think of everything you own as something that is nice to have, but that you could live without. It is to never trade your power to make decisions with property or status. For the stoic, life is not a contest. The contest is to keep your words, deeds, and thoughts united with nature. Whatever else comes your way, as long as you preserve your integrity, is a win. You may lose your house, friends, health, or status but you can still claim victory, even think of those losses as an advantage, if you pass the test of virtue.

Contemplate the death of your heroes

A stoic will recognize that the person many people call a 'loser' may not always be one. Since virtue is the only good, then the loser is the one who does not maintain virtue, not the one who does not have goods, status, or money. But the stoics did not leave it there. They understood that human frailty can trick you into inverting your priorities and so they advised regular meditation on the death of your heroes. That way, you inoculate yourself from the tendency of human nature (and other external factors) to corrupt your pursuit for virtue.

The stoics had heroes like Socrates, Plato, Diogenes, Heracles, Patroclus, Odysseus, and so forth. Their heroes were people who embodied virtue. Today, your heroes may be people who live the kind of life you want to live or who have achieved things that move you. Epictetus recommended that you regularly think about their end of life. In doing so, you balance your perspective. You realize that even the best of us are men at best, which loosens your grasp on material things. If your hero is dead, then you can remind yourself that not so long after their achievements, they died. If alive, then you would remember that one day, they will die. Bear this in mind every day and it will guide you on what you should truly care about.

Do your circumstances in life control you?

Caring less means that you give yourself the freedom from being assailed by circumstance. You start to hold out a place of honor in yourself so that you can take refuge in your inner citadel when circumstance changes. You do this by:

- Becoming a loser.
- Contemplating the death of your heroes.

16

THEIR OPINIONS DO NOT MATTER

'The person who lives as he wishes, who cannot be compelled, impeded or coerced, whose impulses cannot be thwarted, is truly free. He gets what he desires and never has to deal with what he would rather avoid.' –
Epictetus

How often have you entered a meeting and left wondering what the people you met think about you? How many times has the fear of other people's opinions paralyzed you? Have you allowed yourself to change your actions based on what you thought others would feel or say? Historically, the opinions of others played a significant role. Back then, when we were hunters and gatherers, you needed to rely on other people's opinions to be safe. We needed people like us because there was always the possibility of getting thrown out of the tribe or death. You were better off if you did your job and stayed aligned with everyone else. Anyone rebelling against the status quo became an outcast, which meant dying alone. But life has changed and you no longer need other people's opinions to live. So why do you still enslave yourself to the opinions of others? The stoics have something to say about this:

Update your mental model of life

Unlike back then when we survived on fruits and meat and we knew everyone we interacted with, today, the internet connects us on a global scale. More than 40% of the world population can access the internet. Email, social media, and other technology keep us connected at levels our reptilian brain cannot process. That brain still craves being liked even though it will not be outcast by the tribe. By design, it cares about other people's opinions even though that prevents us from performing our best. It becomes a hindrance.

Essentially, you are operating on a flawed or outdated mental model for life. According to Epictetus, true freedom is being able to do what you want, when you want, without being coerced or impeded by others – of course, within the limits of what is right. Working to please everyone is impossible. Everyone will always have their opinions of life and the way things should be. Sometimes, those opinions will oppose yours. This does not mean that you should stop sharing your opinion.

Focus on your actions

Does it really matter what others say? To the extent that everyone matters, then what everyone says matters. But what everyone says must never dictate what you do or overrule what you have to say. So maybe people tell you that they dislike your ideas. Or perhaps, they gossip about you behind your back. Does it really matter? According to Epictetus, the answer is 'no.' You can remind yourself of the typical Epictetus response – 'if they really knew my flaws and who I am, they would have said worse.'

The idea here is to shrug off other people's opinions and instead concentrate on bettering yourself. You could respond to those people. You could try to convince them to see you differently, but it is really what you do that speaks, not just your words. Opposition is natural. It happens to everyone. In fact, if you go through life without opposition, according to Seneca, you will never know what you could do. There are better things to focus on than opposition – your actions. Marcus Aurelius said that peace comes when you stop giving mental space to what others say, think, or do. Focus on what you do and let that speak for you.

∾

How free are you?

The truly free person, as Epictetus puts it, never has to deal with things they would rather avoid. So, there you have it:

- Update your mental model for life and
- Focus on your actions,

-if you want to overcome slavery to the opinions of others. In case you are thinking that it is not as simple as that, in the next chapter, I will give you more reasons not to worry about the opinions of others. For now; how have you been enslaving yourself to the opinions of others?

17

REASONS NOT TO WORRY
WHAT OTHERS THINK

'He gains much time, he who does not consider what his neighbor says, thinks, or does, but only what he himself does, to make it holy and just.' – **Marcus Aurelius**

As far as the stoics were concerned, worrying about the opinion of others is a waste of time. Most people care about the opinions of others, but if you do it to the extent where you disregard yours or make choices that hurt you, then it can be tough on your well-being. To find confidence and happiness, you have to find validation from within. Here are five reasons from the stoics why you should not worry about what others think:

What others think does not change your intrinsic value

Seneca said it best – what they think is just a thought in their mind. That's all. Other people's thoughts about you do not change who you are. If I am being honest, though, this easy truth is difficult to implement because we, by nature, seek the approval of others. Our upbringing conditions us for this – our parents celebrate the child who does what they like. At school, teachers celebrate compliance. Later on, when we start working, our co-workers follow the script as they always did. Few people ever pause to consider the fact that someone's opinion has no effect on our intrinsic value.

Do you become a worse or better person because of someone's thoughts? No, you do not. What others think does not affect your value and your worth. So, if you stop worrying over what others think, you spare yourself the stress. You start to focus on your personal growth. You stop trying to find fault in others as a defense mechanism. You focus on who you want to be.

Your creativity overflows

In the end, you are the only one who chooses who you are. You are the only person who can choose who to become. If someone does not approve of your choices or does not like you, it does not change who you are. When this reality hits home, you realize that no one can hold you back even in your creativity and imagination. You connect with the things that inspire and drive you, and everything only goes uphill from there.

You define success by your internal standards

I must mention here that the idea of caring less is not to completely disregard the opinions of others. It is that if you do listen to others, you do it out of choice, not compulsion, and you consider the things they say only if they are true. So how do you do this? How do you deny the opinions of others sway over you? How do you let it go when someone disparages you? How does praise not go to your head? Spend time clarifying your goals so that you become more in touch with the things you want in life. Once you know the path you are on, it will not matter what others think about it. The clearer your path, the more you stop worrying about other people's opinions, and the more you stop worrying about the opinions of others, the clearer your path will be. It is all connected.

Other people have baggage

In that moment when you are worrying about someone else's opinion, you elevate them to a higher position than yourself. You forget their humanity. The truth of the matter is that other people project their issues onto us. Sometimes they are not even aware that they are doing it. If you worry about what they think, you are wasting your time because they could be criticizing you based on a personal choice they regret. The trick here is to be curious about the verifiable facts and to let go of what you cannot verify.

Imagine you are giving a presentation at work. No one says anything during the meeting but afterwards, you overhear a colleague say they did not like your presentation. Are you to take offense? Does their opinion change your presentation? No. Now imagine you go up to them and ask what they did not like about your presentation. They say they would have used a different PowerPoint background. Or perhaps, an image you used was particularly triggering. These things are just opinions and they are things you cannot change.

However, imagine they told you that your presentation was not well researched. Maybe they saw a graph that was not accurate. These are things you can verify and things you can actually change. You can do more research next time and you can correct your graph. In this case, your response should be gratitude that your colleague was honest with you. The skill the stoics advocated for is learning how to separate opinion from fact. The next time you watch news, pick a paper and divide it into two columns – one for opinions and the other for facts. Listen to the speaker and write down what you hear in the different columns. Notice how many things they say as facts that really are just opinions. This exercise will help you master the stoic skill of differentiating opinion from fact.

You control your own feelings

When you worry about other people's opinions, you are not really in control of your feelings. They are. You have given up control over your internal world to them. If you ever find yourself blaming people for making you feel a certain way about who you are, then you need to take charge. You decide your response to other people's words. Choose instead to learn and grow.

What are you attaching your self-worth to?

The Buddhists teach that all suffering comes from attachment. If you attach your self-worth to what others think, you are setting yourself up for true suffering. You are making yourself a victim. Let's recap the reasons to let go of other people's opinions as seen in this chapter:

- What they think does not change who you are.
- Other people have baggage.
- You define what success means to you.
- Your creativity overflows.
- You gain back control over your feelings.

18

RECOVERING FROM A
BREAKUP

*'Never say of anything 'I have lost it' but, 'I have
returned it.'*
– Epictetus

I
t happens to the best of us. Today we are
happy as a couple, deeply in love, and
holding hands as we make our way to our
favorite spot and the next day, there is a spat. A
mistake is made. Someone arrives late. A harsh
word is said and soon enough, we have to figure
life out without someone we have grown to love.
So, what now? What do you do when the tapestry
of your relationship is torn? Again, the stoics had
something to say about healing from a breakup.

I must mention here that the concept of romance and love has changed across decades. In ancient Greece, the dating culture was vastly different from how we date today. Nonetheless, some human emotions like anger, attachment, craving, love, and lust have not changed. Unlike us, nature has time. So, even though civilization has made leaps and bounds forward, our physiology has not changed much. That is why stoicism can still help us deal with heartbreak. True, we know more now about the way the brain works, but that does not invalidate ancient wisdom.

Before digging into that though, we have to deconstruct what is happening after a breakup and why it feels so bad. Falling in love is very intense. Your body produces chemicals that make you feel good. Soon enough, you can only think about the person you love. These chemicals help you bond. They go by many names, including the 'honeymoon phase.' After that phase wanes, your view of the other person becomes more realistic, but your attachment to them is deep. It is what a breakup interferes with. The question then is; do you have to suffer forever? (It often feels that way). The answer is 'no.' The stoics thought that the rational mind can help you with heartbreak.

Change your beliefs

Even though you cannot wish the pain away, changing some beliefs will make the reality of the breakup easier to deal with. It will make you at peace with your new reality. Here are some of the beliefs you can change according to the stoics:

- **I need them to be happy**

This belief can sometimes manifest as clinginess. In today's world, people simply tell you that 'there are plenty of fish in the sea.' Even though it is true, it is not easy to accept after a breakup. You cannot imagine how someone could possibly want you to replace your beloved. Besides, that saying does not solve the problem. No matter how many fish there are, the fish is still an external reality. In theory, it is possible to never catch any one of those fish even though there are many. It is something you cannot control.

If you suffer after a breakup because you believe you need your ex-partner to be happy, then the mistake you are making is thinking that your happiness depends on the external. Stoicism could not disagree with this more. The stoics believed that the only thing you need to be happy in life is virtue. If that is true, then a relationship, marriage, and romance are unnecessary for your happiness. They are unreliable factors. Concentrate on living a virtuous life and you will be happier.

- **I am entitled to them**

Most of the time, you do not realize when you have subscribed to this idea, but somewhere, along the way, you start to see the person you love as an entitlement. You forget that their time and their love is a gift. This idea often accompanies the fear of loss and jealousy. So, when they break up with you, you feel wronged. You find the reason for the breakup to be unjust. If it is a divorce, you might feel wronged because your former spouse changed their mind about being with you till death do you part. If cheating was involved, you feel betrayed.

The strange part is that sexual exclusivity and monogamy have not always been the norm. They are concepts imposed on social structures and are often handed down alongside religious beliefs. Unchecked, they end up fueling your fear of loss and sense of entitlement. The stoic philosopher

Epictetus had something to say about dealing with this idea after a breakup. According to him, you have not lost love, simply returned it. Whoever gives also has a right to take away. If you think of your ex-spouse that way, you are less likely to feel wronged because they ended things.

- **I will never get over them**

The pain of a breakup makes it seem impossible to get over your ex-partner, but it really is true that time heals all wounds. Marcus Aurelius put it this way – some things are rushing us into life and others out of it. Some of what is now has already passed. Change constantly remakes the world, the way the unrelenting passage of time makes eternity. The pain you feel is something you can work with. You do not have to fight it. You can simply acknowledge it and give it time. Remember that grief is a combination of actively engaging with the world and quietly sitting with it. Embrace what you feel, endure the detachment it will provoke, and let time do its job.

Seneca once wrote to his mother because she mourned his absence. To console her, he recommended that she give her grief time. 'Nothing is more hurtful than medicine applied too soon,' he said. 'Wait until it exhausts itself by its own violence and being weakened by time, you will be able to bear the remedies that would allow grief to be touched.' Put another way, Seneca was advising his mother to let herself cry. In regards to your heartbreak, let yourself cry. Be human. When the initial shock has passed, apply a bandage to the wound.

Do not make things worse

There is a rule about holes – if you find yourself in one, stop digging. It sounds simple, but most people violate it after a heartbreak. When you feel wronged, what do you do? For most people, the first thing is to feel angry and then they flail and make things worse. Seneca thought that we make things worse if we bemoan them. Try not to make your situation worse by introducing anger into the equation. Do not react just because you can. Stop digging. Do not join as many dating apps as you can. Do not rush to be with someone else. Do not take to social media. Remind yourself that you always have a choice. You can focus on how you have been wronged or you can learn and celebrate what was good in the relationship.

Stop looking for a scapegoat

Epictetus spoke harshly against looking for places to cast blame. Rather than crying to God to tell you why your heart had to break, he advises that you stop looking for a scapegoat and do what you need to do. Robert Greene, the author, says that our lives can be divided into two – dead time or alive time. Dead time is when you are passive and waiting while alive time is when you are learning, acting, and redeeming your time. Every minute that you do not choose to control goes either into alive time or dead time. After a breakup, every part of you wants to complain about your circumstances, but this is the attitude that will create dead time. Remember that you can never have that time back. Instead, choose alive time. Shift your speech to 'this is a chance for me to learn and grow.'

Ask for help

It is common for people to feel ashamed about needing help when they are dealing with a breakup. Marcus Aurelius advises that you do not feel ashamed that you need help. You have a duty, like every soldier in battle. If you are injured, you need the help of other soldiers. No one expects you to have all the tools you need to solve all the problems you face. Remember that. Then go ahead and ask for help. You do not need to face everything alone. Simply ask for help.

Focus on the present

After a breakup, your reflection on life can crush you. Listen to Marcus Aurelius and do not fill your mind with every bad thing that could potentially happen. Focus on your present and ask yourself how you can survive it. Just think about it – what were the scariest, most threatening things that you endured in the past? How did you overcome them? You will find that you overcome by seeing past the poor odds. Even here, when your heart reels from heartbreak, do not fill your mind with negativity. Zoom in and look at the details of life – the big picture might be over-whelming in the face of grief. When you focus on the present, you remove the negative thoughts from your mind. It is like this: a man walking a tightrope does not think about how far up he is or how far the end is. He simply puts one foot in front of the other.

Always love

This is arguably the most radical stoic tip for dealing with heartbreak – love. Seneca said it this way – if you would be loved, love. During a heartbreak, it is easy to hate because hate puts off blame. It takes away your responsibility. It distracts you so that you will not do much else when you are busy revenging or exploring the wrongs of others. But does this get you closer to peace of mind? No. It only keeps you in a loop.

The better response is to love. Love the person who let you down. Love the group that rejected you. Love the partner who took your heart carelessly. Love them all because in the end, the love you take is the love you make. Be inspired by men like Martin Luther King Jr., who preached love as freedom and hate as a burden. Hate is a cancer that eats at your very existence. It is a strong acid that erodes the very best of who you are. There is no situation in life where hate makes things better. Yet, love makes almost everything better. And who knows, maybe you will get back some of the love you give.

Are you stuck in a loop, blinded by heartbreak?

I have taken the time to talk about heartbreak because of the way it blinds us. A breakup hides from view everything you know to be important. Yet, we are infinitely adaptable and elastic. We can use stoic wisdom to learn and grow from breakups by:

- Changing your beliefs.
- Not making things worse.
- Taking responsibility.
- Asking for help.
- Focusing on the present, and
- Always choosing love over hate.

19

HOW TO NOT GET OFFENDED

'Anyone who can anger you masters you; he can anger you because you allow yourself to be disturbed by him.'
– Epictetus

The stoics taught that offense is a choice – if you decide not to be offended by what others do, you will not be. Offense is based on your interpretation. Rather than taking offense, you can treat others kindly and assert your autonomy. An example of this in action is a story told about Mahatma Gandhi in South Africa. Gandhi and his friend Charles Freer Andrews were walking in a suburb in Johannesburg. They were accosted by people shouting discriminatory chants at them. Despite Andrews' misgivings, Gandhi kept going, choosing to turn the other cheek. One of the guys shouted 'we are cleaning up our neighborhood,' to which Gandhi responded, 'you will find that there is room for us all.'

You may not be dealing with such racial discrimination like Gandhi, but chances are that you have many other chances to take offense. The information age has given us incredible access to information. You can take university courses online. You can learn art, philosophy, and coding. You can fix your boiler using a YouTube tutorial. There is so much learning potential in today's world. But all this connectedness has a downside. We are more connected with other people's opinions than we were before.

It turns out that argument, debate, and disagreement capture our attention easily. We love the back and forth. We enjoy picking teams. On some level, this is primitive. So much so that some people blind themselves to objective truth in favor of their chosen side. These days, news outlets are competing with sites they never would have imagined to be a threat before – thanks to Facebook, Instagram, and YouTube. People are not interested in conventional news outlets. With all these, offense jumps easily to our minds. You scroll through Instagram and catch a photo that offends you. A YouTube video criticizes something you love and you take offense. Differences in opinion create friction. The result? An outrage culture. But how do you escape from it? The stoics have a way to live a happier life:

Depersonalize opinions

Being offended happens when you identify too strongly with someone else's opinion. It happens when you take someone's opinion so personally it seems like an attack. Yet, most times, unless the opinion is of you, it is just an opinion. A way to deal with taking offense is; when someone voices their opinion, remind yourself that it is not personal. They are simply explaining what they value. A difference in values is not an attack. Values are made on learning and experience. So, at most, such a difference is a mark of a different life.

When you learn to depersonalize opinions, it means that you can have a healthy debate on things like football, religion, nuclear power, and so forth, without getting offended. You can do this because you know that when someone's opinion differs from yours, it is simply because they are articulating their beliefs. Besides, someone's opinion is not necessarily the truth or the reality. It is often just their perspective, based on their life experiences.

Accept the differences

The outrage culture is characterized by a desire to change other people's opinions. It is as if to say that you cannot disagree and live within the same space. Have you seen videos of people getting upset over social movements? Many modern activists may come from a good place, but their execution makes their movement counterproductive. Shouting and screaming are not effective ways to change people's minds. Part of not taking offense is accepting that differences in opinion are okay. You have no authority over other people's opinions, so, if you want to change them, raise your argument, not your voice. Outrage only breeds outrage and causes more suffering. The next time someone voices an opinion you do not agree with, see it for what it is and rather than getting angry and defensive, try to understand where they are coming from.

Master yourself

Ultimately, not getting offended is about mastering yourself. Marcus Aurelius advised compassion for people who offend you. According to him, when others injure you, ask yourself what good you could draw from it – it will draw sympathy from you. You will see that your sense of good and evil may differ from theirs, in which case they deserve compassion. When you choose to get offended, strength dissipates. You start to harbor malice. Kindness, on the other hand, is invincible. Only make sure that it is sincere.

Marcus Aurelius goes on to ask a question: what can a vicious person do if your response is always kind, gently setting him straight? What happens if you show him the way without pointing fingers? Epictetus advocated self-management and integrity as the antidote against taking offense. It may be true that someone should not have treated you a certain way, but that is for them to see. Yours is to act rightly with regard to him. This should be your concern.

How often do you get offended?

Since being offended is a choice you make, not taking offense is an exercise in mastering yourself. The next time you have cause to take offense, choose not to be upset. Try to isolate the offense. Overlook their wrongdoings with compassion and remind yourself that you can only change your own self. It is to your credit if you can overlook an offense. Choose not to let others control you. Now then, let's recap what the stoics have to say about taking offense:

- Other people's opinions are an expression of their values, not something to be taken personally.
- It is okay for people to disagree.
- Offense is a choice. Choose compassion instead.

20

THREE STOIC WAYS OF LETTING GO

'A philosopher expects all hurt and benefit from himself. A proficient one censures no one, accuses no one, praises no one, and blames no one.' – **Epictetus**

I n earlier chapters, we established that you cannot be at peace without learning to let go. We have talked at length about letting go of things you cannot control. But how exactly do you let go? Many people are concerned about living a happy life but they have no idea how. Stoic wisdom has three exercises and wisdom inspired by how the world works to help you live happily. They include:

Change your judgments

The stoics believed that nothing that happens to you or in your environment is inherently good or bad. Events have no moral charge. It is your mind that assigns goodness or badness. Why does this matter? Because most of the things happening in our lives are things we cannot control. All we can control is our ability to judge. Epictetus argued that experiences affect us depending on how we judge them. If you adopt a mind state that is conformable to nature, then you will live happier. Watch your judgments about things you cannot control.

Live well

Virtues and vices have always been part of stoic ethics. They are connected to the stoic idea of living in accordance with nature. If it goes against nature, it is vice. If it aligns with nature, it is virtue. Virtue will always lead to happiness. If you want to learn to let go, live by wisdom, moderation, courage, and justice. When it comes to the large gray area between the good and bad, then judge by wisdom and apply the pursuit of virtue to your choices.

Lower your expectations

High expectations trick us into expecting a desirable outcome from things we cannot control. If you take such a position toward life and toward external things, you will certainly be disappointed. For example, if you expect your father to be supportive, affectionate, and respectful of your decisions, and if instead he is flaky, cold, and disrespectful, you will be disappointed. The question is: are you disappointed because of your father or because of your expectations?

According to Epictetus, you are not entitled to the good. You are not entitled to everything you wish for but only to what is yours by nature. If you expect more than nature offers, you suffer. This suffering will be self-imposed. Marcus Aurelius had similar thoughts. In his lifetime, he had to deal with difficult people and he knew too well that an overly optimistic outlook would set him up to be disappointed. At the beginning of each day, he prepared himself by expecting disloyalty, ill-will, ingratitude, and selfishness from others. This is a good exercise to help you calibrate your expectations so that you are less disturbed by the things that come your way.

What are you holding onto that is not yours to carry?

What things are you clinging to that cause emotional pain? How are you making your suffering worse? According to the stoics, you can learn to let go by:

- Managing your expectations,
- Living virtuously, and
- Changing your judgments of events and the world.

PART IV

MASTER YOUR MIND

21

STOIC WISDOM FOR MENTAL TOUGHNESS

'You have power over your mind – not outside events. Realize this, and you will find strength.' – **Marcus Aurelius**

Have you ever felt as if you were below standard? Has it ever occurred to you that you do not believe you could win in life? Do you live in worry and concerns, probably overwhelmed by everything that has been laid on your shoulders? Do you sometimes second-guess your decisions? If you answered yes to any of these questions, chances are that you are a victim of a weak mental resolve. The best thing for you to do now is to leave your comfort zone and work on your mental strength.

269

A mentally tough person can stand against and manage doubts, worries, and other circumstances that hinder his ability to succeed. They are like a fortress against any setbacks. We all experience fear sometimes. It is a normal part of the human experience, but only the mentally weak live in fear. Mental toughness will give you the ability to deal with challenges and face your fears. No wonder there is a common encouragement for athletes to remain firm and consistent even under pressure. Essentially, the encouragement is for them to be mentally strong. But is mental strength only a reserve for athletes?

What sets apart the truly great people in history from the rest of the population is the will to keep going when others start giving up. It is their ability to see their convictions through even during the hardest of times. It is their persistence despite adversity, and this persistence requires mental toughness. It requires that they embrace uncertainty and discomfort as they negotiate their way forward. Anyone who commits to develop this skill can be truly great.

Bear in mind that greatness is not always synonymous with what the society typically applauds as success. Seneca explains it this way – success comes to the poorly talented and the lowly, but the truly special thing about the great person is their ability to triumph over the panics and disasters of human life. The point here is that you can be born into advantage and seem successful in the eyes of others without making any significant progress of your own.

If you want to be more than a shell, if you want to grow the substance that sets apart the genuinely successful, you need to cultivate the endurance to stick it out. You need the ability to handle rejection and to embrace long periods of hard learning. There are simply no shortcuts. In the end, the only way to develop mental toughness is by learning how to deal well with the obstacles that come your way. Mental toughness is hard won. The best part is that once you cultivate it, the playing field shifts in your favor. You only need to find what is sustainable and what is worth working on to the end. As it turns out, the stoics also understood the incalculable value of this ability. They offer wisdom on developing greater resilience, including:

Get resourceful

Epictetus did not believe in telling his students what they should do. What advice can anyone really give you if they do not understand all the circumstances of your life? – and no one ever does. According to him, the better thing is to teach your mind to be adaptable. A mind that can make peace with any circumstance will take you off-script. It will not be desperate for direction from anywhere. It will find its own path. Our modern education system has rigid structures. Every course has a syllabus and every class has procedures. You are deemed the best if you can learn to be structured. Yet, the minute you step out of the classroom, you find out that life is not as controlled.

At work, for example, circumstances change all the time. In the morning, you start working on a project and by mid-morning, a news event has triggered circumstances so much that you have to change course. It is a major disadvantage if your mind cannot handle ambiguity. If you cannot function without getting specific tasks assigned; if you must get explicit instruction, you will suffer, not just in your office, but in life. There are, after all, no scripts to life. Life is more about resourcefulness than it is about a checklist with prescribed actions. No single blueprint works.

Even if you designed your life after the life of someone you admire, there would still be so many variables and so much nuance that you would need to be resourceful. You cannot escape it. You have to learn to adapt and to make your own momentum even when you meet challenges. Every day gives you an opportunity to learn how to make things work regardless of your situation. Mental strength is about leveraging the experience you have gained through life to be resourceful.

Spend time alone

Seneca thought that a man's ability to stop his plans and pass time alone is the surest mark of a well-ordered mind. Nothing could be truer. Most of the time, a chaotic and undisciplined mind camouflages as busyness. To build mental strength, learn to be content spending time alone. Embrace introspection. It is the only way for you to know what truly matters to you and what you want to make of your life. The sooner you do this, the more focused you will be.

Introspection will also help you to connect with yourself and work 'in the zone.' The much desired 'flow' is a product of a quiet and focused mind. Those who bounce between distractions are not capable of cultivating the resilience they need to set themselves apart. Create a place in your mind where you can retreat to, quiet any noise around you, and throw yourself into your work. Prioritize alone time and you will become more stable and resilient.

Consume less, create more

Many people cannot handle how tiresome and demanding sustained immersion in any field of study is. Few people can live with doing the same thing over and over. Others never even consider starting because they fear the demands. They end up picking distractions and illusions over their dreams. The flip side is that they never realize the pleasures reserved for those who choose to master themselves and their craft. There is no mental strength without a commitment to see whatever you start to the end. If it is your own business or creating your own art, whatever it is, it will call to you to keep showing up every day.

It is easier to give up. There are all kinds of reasons to tap out, but in doing so, you betray yourself. You leave the creation of meaning to everyone else but you. Because as the stoics saw it, what you create and what you put out into the world is what will define you.

What defines you?

In what ways are you betraying yourself and your vision for distractions and illusions? What have you committed to? According to the stoics, you build mental strength by:

- Spending time alone.
- Cultivating resourcefulness.
- Creating more than you consume.

22

WHEN LIFE HURTS, STOP CLINGING TO IT

'It is not insults or ill language that is insulting, but the principle interpreting them. When anyone provokes you, be assured that it is your own opinion that provokes you.' – **Epictetus**

E pictetus observed that we get burdened in life because we care about too many things. His advice was to care less – stop caring about things that do not matter, only care for the right things. But then, how do you decide what matters and what doesn't? As it turns out, what matters is bound by our perceptions of our place in an environment that is always changing. Undeniably, though, whatever your perceptions, there are things you can change and things you cannot change. Caring about what you can change gives you strength while caring about what you cannot change disempowers you. It gets worse if you cling to those disempowering things.

Part of mental toughness is knowing when to let go and when to hold on, but it is a complicated thing to know when to let go. In one example, Epictetus talked about going to exile. Nothing prevented him from getting exiled with a smile – yet, if he had clung to the idea of exile being a tragedy, he would have been in agony. He understood well where his choices ended and where other people's begun. He chose not to care about what was not his to choose. A simple summary of his philosophy is this – let go of what you cannot control, do not cling to what hurts. He provided methods to do this, including:

Don't cling to borrowed goods

It seems natural to get attached to people we spend a lot of time with, and to objects. Continually, we introduce a possessive element to love and attachment. Then, when someone leaves our presence, for example, we feel hurt and deserted. And what's worse, we lose the person many times in our minds before we even lose them in reality, because of the constant fear that they would leave. Our imagination is deceitful that way. Clinging to something or someone exposes you to the continual hurt of dealing with the possibility of their departure. In some cases, you are so afraid of losing them that your life becomes about preventing the separation. This cycle is also true for power.

The Greek philosopher Epicurus, talking about power, said that it is insatiable. No wonder, when you get some power, you hunger for more. We get corrupted by power and it causes us misery and suffering because we want more or do not want to give it up. The irony is that even if power makes you think you are in control, you are not. Power can be taken and given at any time. This is why it is a fool who fights for it. If you want to live like the stoics, in accordance with nature, you have to adjust to impermanence.

Think of people, power, and objects the way Epictetus did – as a dinner party. In a dinner party, when something is brought before you, you pick it in moderation and pass the rest. You do not stop the flow of events. It never even occurs to you to. When a glass of wine does not come your way, you wait for it and it eventually does.

Do this with people, power, and objects. Living in alignment with nature is going with the flow. If people come to you, accept them with love. If they leave, love them still but let them go. If you get objects and power, embrace them. If they are taken away, such is life.

This attitude will toughen you against the pain of loss. It will change your perceptions about the things you love. Rather than imagining that you own something or are entitled to it, see it all as borrowed. If your loved one passes on, appreciate the time you spent with them and accept that they have returned. This attitude will also help you to take care of what you have while you have it. After all, you are just a traveler in a hotel. Clinging to what is borrowed will only cause you pain. Live in such a way that you can let go of what you have at any time.

Don't cling to other people's opinions

Many people will do whatever they can to be liked by others. It is worse in today's world of technological connectivity. True, there are benefits to people thinking well of us. For example, if we are likable, we can make friends easily. If we are attractive, it may be easier to find a romantic partner and so forth. But, according to the stoics, outside factors should always bow to our equanimity. We should not be grieved when we do not get an invitation to a party, for example, and more so if we do not like the host. Getting invited has benefits – like attendance and praise – but if we are unwilling to invest energy and time interacting with a certain person, then we should have no issues if we are not invited. There are no two ways about it.

Regardless of how happy it makes you feel in the moment, the pursuit of being liked is exhausting. You do not praise people you would rather not be with for the sake of inner peace. In fact, that very thing is mutually exclusive with tranquility. According to Epictetus, we must be willing to be despised and ridiculed if that is the price for tranquility, freedom, and equanimity. We must be happy to be thought stupid if we are at peace because at the end of the day, other people's opinions are not something we can control. We can only control how they affect us. When you cling to people's opinions, you let yourself be guided by them and of what benefit is that to you?

~

Don't cling to ideas and outcomes

You lose every time you try to control the universe. Try to change what is, and you will lose that battle too. Yet, most of the time, we occupy ourselves with what should be happening in the present, what the past should have looked like, and what we expect of the future. The more we resist what is, though, the more life will hurt. Regarding this idea, Epictetus tells us the way we should treat a servant. A servant should be obedient, but he should conduct himself in such a way that he must not always obey. People are people and it is normal to not always behave as expected. The point Epictetus was trying to make is that if we accept that the servant will not always behave as we wish, then we will be at peace. This idea can apply to anything.

For example, you cannot always expect the world to be kind. Some people will be offensive in your eyes. Silencing them will not change the fact that someone will always offend someone else. That is the nature of humanity. So, entertaining the idea of an inoffensive world will set you up for disappointment, and imposing it will only do harm. A better approach is to start being kind to yourself, which is something you can control. Other people may follow your example, but that is up to them. The comings and goings of the world are not ours to determine. If we cling to them, we lose. If we accept them and live well anyway, we win.

Epictetus taught the art of letting go. He taught that you will be happier and stronger if you do not cling to:

- Ideas and outcomes.
- The opinions of others.
- Borrowed goods.

23

BUILD MENTAL FORTITUDE

'When you arise in the morning, think what a precious privilege it is to be alive – to breathe, to think, to enjoy, to love.'
– Marcus Aurelius

Sometimes people mistake isolation with having fortitude. There is a huge difference between the two though. When you isolate, you separate yourself physically, looking for a fortress to hide from the big and terrifying things in the world. Serial self-isolators end up feeling powerless and helpless, believing that whatever is happening outside their fortress is too much for them to handle. They believe they lack the skill and the strength to cope. Unfortunately, they end up missing out on many experiences in life because they are afraid to face malevolence.

Rather than self-isolation, you could choose strength. You could choose to fortify your faculties and make yourself better able to handle unpleasant situations and people. That way, no bad thing will stop you from living a good life. The stoics advocated for this way of living in the world. To them building fortitude was about building the strength of mind to live a good life. Based on stoic principles, you can strengthen your mind to become less inclined to hide away when you sense trouble and to live your life fully. Here are some of those principles:

Examine your beliefs about life

We all have some beliefs that govern the way we live. Some of them are the reason we are upset by life events, making our life so hard that it seems unbearable. As Seneca put it, it is not life itself, but our beliefs that cause us pain. The logic behind it is that we tend to connect our happiness with certain expectations and when they go unfulfilled, we suffer. Writing a letter to his friend Serenus, Seneca explored this idea further.

Serenus wished that people would not be rude to each other. Seneca explained to him that his perspective was wrong. Serenus was wishing that the whole human race be kind, which is impossible.

Like Serenus, we often need to change the way we look at the world. In making such a change, we avoid the unnecessary pain of resistance. Life is filled with violent, selfish, and rude people. When we accept this fact, we can face life in a peaceful way. Seneca went on to say that we cannot live well if we do not know how to die well. As far as he was concerned, mental fortitude is tied to the realization that death is inevitable. When you know that you could die anytime, nothing will surprise you.

Curb your aversions and desires

According to Epictetus, mental fortitude is founded on restraining our aversions and desires. Most people begin their day or enter situations hoping for certain outcomes. This is not always bad, but it has consequences. For Epictetus, the man who defers desire and uses his aversion only on things he can control is truly happy and at peace. This is true for every area of life. Think about it – things that you cannot control are slavish. When your mood depends on them, it is always unstable. Epictetus advised that we adopt an indifferent view toward anything that we cannot control. Mental fortitude is about building a healthy contempt for what you cannot control. In practice, this looks like not desiring the applause and approval of people, not being averse to losing possessions, and focusing only on your actions.

Do only good

Chrysippus is considered one of the greatest stoics. He wrote over 700 volumes but unfortunately, none of them survived. However, his ideas lived on. He expanded on the stoic ethical system, introducing the idea that all our actions are geared toward living a happy life. To get there, we should know what is good from what is bad, and do only good. Of course, this demands courage, which is one of the elements of building stoic fortitude. Most of the time, to do good, you must face your fears and deal with pain. Courage allows you to do right and work toward your goals.

As it will happen often, when you are tempted to pursue vice, you will need courage to resist. Vice promises pleasure but that pleasure is short term. Inevitably, it makes things worse for you and for everyone around you. On the other hand, virtue may be temporarily uncomfortable, but its satisfaction is long term and worth it. If you adopt this mindset, you will be stronger during adversity. You will learn not to let the external overshadow your ability to choose to do good.

What do you believe about life and how does it help your mental wellbeing and strength?

To summarize it all, stoic mental fortitude is about three things:

- Letting go of our ideas of the way the world should be and accepting what is.
- Staying indifferent to anything independent of our will.
- The courage to do good.

24

STOIC WAYS TO OVERCOME THE CHAINS OF THE MODERN WORLD

'If all geniuses in history focused on this one theme, they could never fully explain how baffled they are by the human mind. No one would surrender their estate and the smallest dispute with a neighbor would breed chaos; yet, very easily, we allow others to encroach our lives. Worse, we create the way for them to take over. No one gives their money to a passerby, but how often do we hand over our lives to others! We hold on to our money and property and think little of wasting time, the one thing we should all be miserly about.' –
Seneca

You may not be someone's slave in the sense that Epictetus was, but the modern world has chains of its own. When I speak of chains in this chapter, I do not mean a specific religious, cultural, or political system even though the scope could reach there. I mean the world underneath it all – the slavery to the whims of our environment. I mean, look at how humanity has made decisions in the past. It seems like we are completely controlled by everything around us. When we get the things we hope for, we are happy. When those things are taken away, we get sad. People praise us and we are elated. They dislike us and we become miserable.

It seems as if the more we want something, the more willing we are to sacrifice to get it. The more we oppose something, the more willing we are to pay the costly price to avoid it. These chains are tied to our desires and our dislikes. They control us by fear, blame, manipulation, and shame, leaving us open to manipulation by anyone who would be willing, from large companies to political parties – as long as we have something they want. So then, the world rules us. We become the proverbial donkey chasing after the carrot on the stick. We follow the rider's carrot from birth to death, never questioning whose music we are dancing to.

But what if we chose to play our own tune? What if we rejected the carrot and broke the chains? Stoicism was concerned with the attainment of freedom from chains like those in our world. That freedom does not come when we destroy our surroundings. The environment is not to blame. The universe will always do what it does, and even though we can exercise some influence, we cannot command it. The way rain or sunshine hits a farmer's crops; is the way the world outside imposes on us its conditions. These conditions are not the chains I speak of. Our attachment to them is.

How is it that whenever things change at work we are filled with worry? How come even a small misfortune, as small as someone cutting in front of us in traffic, spoils our day? How do the smallest turns of fate play with our emotions like puppeteers? Death, for example, is not a terrible thing – otherwise the stories of people who faced it valiantly like Socrates would not inspire us. If that is the case, why are we terrified of it? The chains keep getting tighter every time we tug at them. Whenever we see blessing and tragedy in what is natural, we let fortune control us. Fortunately, the stoics provided wisdom to help us break our chains. The following are five stoic ideas that will help us replace our erratic mode of living with freedom:

Premeditate the worst – *Premeditation Malorum*

According to Seneca, nothing happens to the wise person that they did not expect. The stoic idea of premeditating the worst is an exercise in imagining all the things that could be taken away from us or that could go wrong. This helps you to prepare for the setbacks that are inevitable in life and to grow in resilience when you are facing uncertainty. We do not always get the things we work hard for. Not everything is as straightforward and good as we hope. That is why we have to prepare for anything.

Seneca went on to say that the things we do not anticipate are the things that crush us. Their unexpectedness adds weight to their misfortune. This is why we should not let anything take us by surprise. Train yourself to project your thoughts ahead of you at every turn. Conceptualize every possible eventuality. Rehearse in your mind things like a shipwreck, war, torture, and so forth. Make sure that all the terms of human experience are before your eyes. By doing this, you will be prepared for difficulty. You will be ready for any fate.

Meditate on the mutual interdependence of all things

The stoics believed that all things in the universe are interconnected and mutually interdependent. They are woven together and so they attract each other. One thing comes after the next, according to their relationship and the unity of all things. This is one of the most radical stoic ideas – the belief that we are all one. You can find this link in the works of Seneca, Marcus Aurelius, and Epictetus. Marcus Aurelius talks about the common good a lot in his book *Meditations*. He self-identifies, not just as a Roman citizen, but as a citizen of the world.

The stoics understood that as long as they remembered the limitations of their individual perspective, they would be better. Marcus Aurelius talked about taking the 'view from above.' The idea is to challenge your preconceptions at the ground level. That way, you see the world around you more empathetically, fairly, and accurately. This is something you can train yourself to do. Also referred to as 'sympatheia,' the invitation is to step back and zoom out so that you can see life from a higher perspective. It will change your judgments of value, weaken the power of temptation and luxury over you, and reduce the differences between races and people. It will also turn down the worries of your daily life. Try it and see.

Remember the highest good

According to Marcus Aurelius, the highest good in life is truth, justice, self-control, and courage – otherwise, virtue. It is the sufficiency of the mind that helps you to act according to reason and accept the hand of fate outside your power to choose. The highest good is what you are supposed to be aiming for in life. According to the stoics, if you live a virtuous life, you will be happy, successful, honorable, reputable, and your life will be full of meaning.

The claim here is not that remembering and pursuing the highest good will be easy. The stoics had no illusions that it would be. In fact, that path may not even be recognized or celebrated by the people around us. But it is essential for you to be mentally strong and at peace. The alternative – taking the immoral and unethical path – will only breed misery and is the cup reserved for fools and cowards, according to the stoics. If you let virtue lead you every step of the way, your path will be safe.

The ego is the enemy

According to Zeno, nothing is more hostile to knowledge than self-deception. Self-deception and delusions of grandeur are not just inconvenient and annoying traits. Ego is more than being obnoxious and unpleasant to be around. It is the sworn enemy to growth, learning, and progress. It is the overgrown sense of self-importance that blinds you to truth. It is a visceral self-absorption, a belief that you are somehow, by nature, more entitled and better than everyone else. One NBA player described the ego as the 'disease of me.' It is that voice in your ear telling you how invincible you are. For others, it is the voice telling you how everyone is against you. The ego is a toxic force that works against empathy, artistry, vulnerability, and real teamwork.

According to Epictetus, it is impossible for anyone to learn what he already assumes he knows. If you are living in the ego, you are unable to learn, to improve, or to earn the respect of others. You think of yourself as perfect – a genius, deserving the admiration of others. Because of the way it plays with your view of reality, the ego is an enemy of the person you wish you were. The stoics advised that everyone meet the ego with contempt and hostility. We must keep it away, a day at a time. Just think about it: can you identify a situation you were in where you needed more ego? Ego repulses opportunities and advantages and attracts errors and mistakes. Whatever you do in life, keep the ego at bay and you will increase your chances of success significantly.

Remember death - *Memento Mori*

If you have been following the news, you know of all the incredible and sometimes ridiculous things happening in Silicon Valley. Recently, the headlines were flooded with the work of one Peter Thiel. News has it that the man is about to find the key to eternal life. Soon enough, startups will supposedly succeed in granting immortality. One man, reportedly, hopes to 'cure death' while another one thinks no one should accept mortality. Not only are we to live forever, these men believe that we will become part of the singularity. They anticipate a merging between humanity and artificial intelligence to transcend the limitations of being human. If we do not get there quickly enough, we are frozen in liquid nitrogen to be awakened when humans finally achieve immortality.

Then, of course, there is the other side of the story – the skeptics. That side has those who do not believe that humans will be merged with computers. The curious thing though is that even that group would still rather avoid thinking about death. To them, it is scary and unpleasant. It is sad. Why would anyone want to think about something they do not want to happen? The truly wise, though, know that both sides are misguided. They have understood that death is not something to be avoided but embraced, so they act according to this truth.

Seneca advised that we prepare our minds for death. Then, we would postpone nothing. He urged us to balance life's books every day so that everyone puts the finishing touches at the end of each day as though it were the last. The ancient Romans had a tradition where they celebrated victorious generals when they returned. The celebration would be a drawn-out spectacle meant to exalt the leader. On the day of the parade, the leader was required to wear a crown and a gold and purple toga that was only reserved for kings. He would be given a four-horse chariot that would go parting the streets, lined with people chanting about his triumph.

However, in all this pomp and glory, there was also a curious addition. Deliberately positioned in the chariot behind the master, a slave would whisper to him 'memento mori, memento mori.' Otherwise translated it means, 'remember that you are mortal.' The reminder was meant to help the man survive his momentary immortalization without delusions of grandeur.

Lately, people talk about living each day like it was your last so much that it has become cliché. Yet, few people actually live that way, even though that is the essence of remembering death. No, it does not mean that you forsake considerations and laws as if it is the end of the world. What the stoics were saying is that you are a soldier in a battle. You do not know when you will be called to return. You must handle your business. Tell your loved ones that you care. You do not have time to argue over petty issues. You live each day knowing that if it were indeed your last, you would die well.

~

So how are you living your life?

When was the last time you contemplated death? The stoics never divorced a good life with thoughtfulness. If you want to escape the chains of the modern world, you have to:

- Pre-meditate the worst.
- Consider how everything is interconnected.
- Pursue the highest good.
- Kill the ego, and
- Remember death.

AFTERWORD

Few of us would imagine ourselves philosophers. As far as we are concerned, we are nothing like the unexcitable intellectuals in college who would spend countless days studying the philosophical works of men like Karl Marx. Fortunately, we don't have to be that way to enjoy the benefits of stoic wisdom applied to our lives. Stoicism is not concerned with complicated theories of the world and how it operates. It is all about helping us to deal with destructive emotions and to carry ourselves the best way we possibly can.

In this book, I have laid it all out for you. I have worked to make it as clear as possible and as actionable as can be. From this book, you are well aware of how unpredictable the world can be and how little control we have of our fate and of our environment. You are familiar with the brevity of life. Only the strong and the steadfast manage to make much of their time here. Hopefully, you have felt your dissatisfaction understood and addressed. You now know that you do not have to live under the mercy of your emotions, other people's opinions, and things outside of your control.

I have drawn the majority of the lessons and action points from the works of Marcus Aurelius, Seneca, and Epictetus. Zeno the Citium and a few others have also been mentioned here and there. Hopefully, you were able to see how stoicism differs from other existing schools of thought in that it is all about practical application. It is not about intellect. It is a tool that you can use to become a better father, better friend, and a better person. It is not something to beat yourself over or highlight what you lack. It is meditative in its design and transformative in its effect. So then, the question is, are you going to put what you have learnt into practice? Will this be another addition to your knowledge arsenal or will you let it sieve into your heart and produce a change in the way you live? I can tell you for sure that if you let it, the wisdom of the stoics contained in this book will give you a happier life; where you care less and master your emotions the way the stoics did. All the best in that journey!

THANK YOU!

Thank you so much for buying my book.

I know you had many options to pick from but you picked this one.

Because of that, I am grateful. Thank you for reading it to the end. I hope that you have gotten what you came here for and then some.

Before you go, I need to ask for a small favor from you. **Would you kindly post a review of the book? Leaving a review is the easiest and best way to support our work. You can leave an honest review here.**

And you know what? Your feedback helps me to keep writing books like this one that will hold

your hand toward the kind of personal changes you want to make in your life. It would mean the world to me to hear from you.

ALSO BY ALEXANDER CLARKE

Visit my author page

author.to/alexanderclarke

STOP OVER THINKING

The 34 Best Techniques to Reducing Stress, Controlling Your Mind, Overcoming Negative Thoughts and Living a Worry-Free Life

ALEXANDER CLARKE

YOUR FREE GUIDE

To help you control your mind I've created a guide with 9 easy tools from Stoics to build mental strength. Make sure you download it at the following URL:

alexander-clarke.com

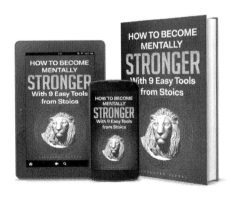

It will help you greatly on your personal development journey. The stronger you train your mind to be, the more you will control your thoughts.

If you want to master your mind and your emotions make sure to grab this free guide!

REFERENCES

Alexander, W. H. (1950). *Lucius Annaeus Seneca. De Beneficiis Libri Vii: The text emended and explained.*

Aurelius, M. (2016). *Marcus Aurelius - Meditations: Adapted for the contemporary reader.* Createspace Independent Publishing Platform.

Bevan, E. R. (1913). *Stoics and skeptics: Zeno of citium and the stoa.*

Bigfield, R. (2017). *Stoicism: Conquer fear, crush stress, find inner peace and be successful.* Createspace Independent Publishing Platform.

Carter, E., & Epictetus. (2017). *The complete works of Epictetus.*

REFERENCES

Epictetus, E., Long, G., & Spalding, J. L. (2015). *Discourses of Epictetus*. Arkose Press.

Epictetus. (2017). *The philosophy of Epictetus: Golden sayings and fragments*. Courier Dover Publications.

McLynn, F. (2010). *Marcus Aurelius: Warrior, philosopher, emperor*. Random House.

Robertson, D. (2018). *Stoicism and the art of happiness: Practical wisdom for everyday life*. Teach Yourself.

Seddon, K. (2008). *A summary of stoic philosophy: Zeno of citium in Diogenes Laertius book seven*. Lulu.com.

Seneca, L. A. (1806). *Seneca's morals by way of abstract*.

THE POWER OF STOICISM

9 LAWS FROM STOICS TO BUILD AN
UNBREAKABLE MIND, FORGE
RESILIENCE, CONQUER YOUR
FEARS, AND BECOME UNSHAKABLE
IN FACE OF ADVERSITY

ALSO BY ALEXANDER CLARKE

Visit my author page

author.to/alexanderclarke

STOP OVER THINKING

The 34 Best Techniques to Reducing Stress,
Controlling Your Mind, Overcoming Negative
Thoughts and Living a Worry-Free Life

ALEXANDER CLARKE

YOUR FREE GUIDE

To help you control your mind I've created a guide with 9 easy tools from Stoics to build mental strength. Make sure you download it at the following URL:

alexander-clarke.com

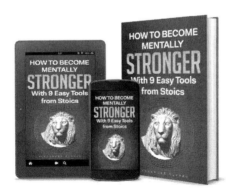

It will help you greatly on your personal development journey. The stronger you train your mind to be, the more you will control your thoughts.

If you want to master your mind and your emotions make sure to grab this free guide!

INTRODUCTION

On a lazy Sunday afternoon, I sat with a friend catching up on life, its fickleness, meaning, and our current pursuits. I was not trying to drive the conversation in any direction, but as such sober discussions often go, we found ourselves pondering death. I was curious about what someone who interacts with its reality more than the average person would say. My friend is a doctor. 'I see many people dying,' he said. 'Some are young, and others are old. Occasionally, it is a child. The most striking thing about all of them, with the rare exception, is that they are afraid of dying.' He seemed lost in thought, and I wanted to see where his thoughts would take us, so I said nothing.

'When an elderly person shows fear of dying, I wonder why, at their age, they are afraid of death. Often, I come up with the same answer – they have unfinished business. They have dreams they have yet to achieve. They still believe that here, under the sun, is something left for them to do or to see, if only they could get a little more time.' He paused. 'I believe that is the worst feeling at the time of death – to know that you could have done more with your life.' I wanted him to shed some more light on that statement, but our conversation flowed in other directions, so I let it go. Still, it remained on my mind.

I have heard people, often young people trying to find their place in the world or people who have been momentarily disillusioned by tragedy, ask this question – why should I do anything? Why should I chase my dreams, for example, if I know that death is imminent? I could die tomorrow; what good is going after your dreams? Later that day, I realized that the answer to that question lies in some of my friend's sentiments. If you are content with the things you have already experienced or achieved at any moment, then you are not afraid of death. Yet, this is often not the case. Often, our imperfections and fallibility as humans stop us from keeping up with the demands of our desires pitted against time.

When we look at life, it can seem that failures outnumber our success rates, however differently we define success – which is the other issue closely tied to the fear of death. When we are successful, and as long as we have determined success to align with our values, then we have moments to cherish and revel in. Although death is inevitable, success produces a feeling that our lives are meaningful, so we accept death's reality with grace. The realization that you tried – maybe even did the best you could, and it panned out well - allows you to leave happily when death calls. The truth of the matter is that we are dying. Death is knocking at your door. It is coming for the people you love. We are constantly faced with our mortality. To live well is to accept that illness will be part of your life and other people's, and it will be terrible. It may take an emotional toll beyond your wildest imagining. It could even be a huge financial blow. That is always a possibility for all people.

Still, our mortality is not the only thing we have to contend with. There is culture and its authoritarian aspects. Here, I am not thinking about a situation where psychopaths and dangerous people hold power and make it miserable for everyone else, even though that is a possible reality. Thankfully though, political tyranny was worse in the past than it is today. Now, people get to design the government systems they live under. Yet, there is much work to be done. The lack of political tyrants does not guarantee a seamless and well-functioning democracy. Corruption, violence, and dysfunction continue to trickle into the culture, and these things influence how you live your life. Culture crushes you. It threatens to turn you into a cog; if it prevails, it may get the best parts of who you are.

As if culture and our mortality are not trouble enough, there is your own shadow. You are a mass of constant contradictions. Think about it – on some days, you know what you should do, but you continually do things that do you no good. You can hardly organize yourself. It is as though you are creating obstacles just so that you can trip over them. In some aspects of your life, you are still a prisoner of your shadow. This is the mental landscape in which this book comes in. I must disclaim that not everyone caves under these challenges similarly. Some people have learned, through difficulties, education, or observation, to do better than others in overcoming trouble. I am saying, though, that man is born into trouble, and to some degree, man must learn to contend with it.

The dark realities that populate our mental landscape can make it appear as though there is no use in trying to overcome them. What use is it to go after the good if darkness still prevails? If death comes for us all, why bother? Over many years of practicing as a coach and counselor and interacting with all kinds of psychological and stoic literature, it has become clear that the solution to the problem is not defeatism, no matter how attractive it sometimes is. Making things worse is not a tenable option. The answer lies in a deeply religious, psychological, and stoic idea – that the voluntary confrontation of the unknown is a cure. The stoics believed it. The founders of psychology taught it, and the greats lived it throughout history.

Then, of course, there are the external challenges - starting a business and dealing with policies and laws that seem to work against you, handling competition. Or it could be that you work in a high-pressure environment and every day, you have to deal with countless expectations from your boss and colleagues. Many years ago, I was going through a personal crisis, and I was stuck in a rut. I found it difficult to believe that I could make anything good out of my life, so a friend shared a story with me. This is the story – a guy was terrified of water. He could not imagine going into a pool. The beach was undoubtedly a no-go zone for him. The situation was so bad that showering and washing his hands felt like torture. Anything connected to water made him want to disappear. This was a phobia he developed in his teens, and it was haunting him way into adulthood.

One day, the guy goes to a party and two guests grab him and push him into the pool. They did not know about his severe water phobia. They just wanted to have a good time at his expense. But the prank went bad at first. The guy started throwing his hands in panic, genuinely afraid for his life. This went on for a few moments. The crowd was no longer excited. Things began to get uncomfortable. Someone was getting ready to jump into the pool to help when the guy realized he could stand on his feet. When he did, the water was less than his height. He was still afraid, but now he could breathe. His head was above the water. He was fine after all. He started to calm down. That was the beginning of the end of his debilitating phobia.

My friend told me the story to show me that sometimes things are not as bad as we think, but I use it to illustrate my point – when we face the obstacles in our path, we grow from them. Like the guy in the story, our anxiety and fears may be unjustified, and the only way to know for sure is to confront the obstacle. Of course, this idea is not new. The stoics believed it. Their teachings promote mental calm in the face of adversity. They recommend bringing our beliefs to question, examining them, and keeping them only if they match reality. For them, the ideal state of mind is not necessarily a positive mind, but a peaceful one of calm indifference toward your circumstances — an unbreakable mind.

That is what I want to offer you in this book. Maybe you are reading this and thinking, 'I am a business leader with too many concerns to be thinking about the things you have mentioned.' If that is you, - and you have to confront not only your mortality and fallibility, but also the issues overwhelming your employees - that is precisely why you need this book. The human mind has an incredible capacity to parallel process – entertaining different feelings and thoughts at once. That is a cursed gift. If you do not train yourself to deal with the cascade of concerns, you may obsess over challenges until they overtake you. You fail to keep perspective, reset, and deal with the challenges.

This book is your psychological toolkit. It has everything you need to deal with your personal challenges and the challenges others face that affect you and your organization. It has everything you need to appreciate the things that are going well when facing adversity. It contains all you need to chart a way out of adversity with resilience. Here, you will learn how to tackle challenges and stay focused – an essential aspect of making resilience both a personal and collective endeavor. Here, you will get a superpower that all business leaders need.

I have designed this book as a mental roadmap to becoming mentally strong. Each chapter builds on to the next. At the end of each chapter, you will find suggestions to help you begin practicing the content you have just interacted with. My goal is to provide you with the theory and tips on how to practice them as you act on your goals. Here, you will find tried and tested tools to learn success principles, habits, and strategies, and implement them in your life in a way that lasts.

I am Alexander Clarke. I have been a practicing counselor and coach for many years. I have a BA in Behavioral Psychology and an MA in Philosophy. Throughout my career, I have had the pleasure of helping business leaders and executives get a handle on the challenges they are facing, regroup, and come back with a clear head to create better solutions for themselves and the people they lead. I have sat across executives grappling with problems whose scope is so broad that failure would affect many people. I have seen them almost cave under their responsibilities. I have also seen them tap into an internal strength they did not know they possessed to stand against incredible difficulties.

I have also had the privilege of academia. I was partly driven by my desire to overcome challenges and partly by the desire to use my knowledge to help others deal with obstacles better. I have read what the Stoics have to say about mental fortitude and resilience and analyzed different stories from people who have had great success implementing stoic philosophy. I have read psychological journals investigating mental strength and researched the chemistry of the mind.

As providence would have it, I have written and published several books in psychology, stoicism, mastering the mind and emotions, and self-discipline, to name a few. This book is not just an addition to the library; it is also unique in its approach. Here, I have whittled down stoic wisdom to nine principles with a laser focus on resilience. I have done everything to provide only that which is valuable and practical. You can implement what you find here today. I know that this book will add real value to your life. It will help you to become unshakeable in the face of adversity.

1

BE STRICT WITH YOURSELF

'Be tolerant with others and strict with yourself'
– Marcus Aurelius.

In 2020, I went out for a networking dinner with a few friends. One of them introduced me to a colleague with the statement, 'This is Alex. He is very strict with his diet.' I was taken aback by the comment. I even found myself needing to explain that I was not strict. I was completely free to choose whatever I wanted to eat, I just happened to want healthy foods. I restrained myself from explaining, though. Saying that I was very strict seemed to suggest that I was depriving myself of something, when I do not really think of my eating habits as a denial. In fact, I feel that I am loving myself when I make healthy choices.

When I meet with friends who take care of their health as much as I do and we have similar diets, it is always enjoyable to exchange ideas and talk about what we are learning. It never feels like denial in any way. I only get perceived as 'very strict' by people who have a different lifestyle. What I considered to be self-discipline and a conscious decision not to give in to unhealthy impulses was interpreted by others as strictness. This made me think about the quote by Marcus Aurelius – be tolerant with others and strict with yourself. What did he mean? What about strictness did he know that I didn't so that when I was described as 'very strict,' it didn't resonate?

After much consideration, I realized that his statement was about self-discipline. The dictionary describes self-discipline as *correcting or regulating yourself so that you can improve*. I initially assumed that strictness is denying or restricting yourself unnecessarily, but the dictionary defines it as following rules or beliefs exactly as they are. This is the definition Marcus Aurelius had in mind. Being strict with yourself is about having willpower because you chose to love all versions of yourself (including the future you, who will be better because of your present choice) enough to desire improvement.

Think about it – it may be that one of the reasons people struggle with self-discipline and willpower is that they imagine they are denying themselves instead of loving themselves and choosing the better option. They do not factor in that they are choosing control over their neural mechanisms and stress when they choose self-discipline. Let me explain. Our bodies are living, breathing systems. They are constantly in flux as they respond to changes within the external and internal environment. When we face a challenge and the body perceives that you do not have what it takes to stay in balance, you experience it as stress.

The physiological response that follows stress kicks in. It is automatic and it triggers many other physiological changes. It is driven by two hormones - adrenaline and cortisol. The changes in the body stimulate negative thoughts and emotions, which drive physical behaviors and actions that are meant to help you find relief or resolution for the problem. When you feel hungry, you respond to the need by finding food to eat. When you are cold, you get a scarf. When your leg starts getting numb, you are motivated to get up.

Ideally, our stress response would be the perfect solution to the problem, but sometimes, we respond to a problem to find relief, not necessarily because the response is appropriate. Imagine someone who gets nervous about not being able to meet their financial responsibilities. Their nervousness causes them to eat. Why would you eat instead of paying your bills? Maybe they do not have the money they need and they are worried. Food takes away the worry for a short while. The fact that they do not have an immediate solution causes an overactive response to stress, which raises their heart rate, increases their stress hormones, and makes the load seem harder to bear, causing them to want immediate relief. Food provides that.

All through your life, you have experienced different stressors which did not have immediate solutions, so you found habits and behaviors that take the bad feeling away – like eating sweet foods, overworking as an escape, smoking, or whatever other habit. These behaviors do not provide a solution, but they help you feel better in the moment. They provide relief by quieting your stress response. They are a coping mechanism. Over time, these habits become default. They automatically kick in whenever you are faced with stress associated with a challenge.

Yet, even though they help you cope with stress, these habits are destructive. They destroy your stress system. For example, if your default coping strategy is to feel guilty, you may feel all the guilt in the world, but it does not help. It will not help you when you are trying to reconcile two conflicting employees, develop a new skill so that you move up in your workplace, or get fit. It will not help you when you are trying to stay the course because you lack the willpower or strictness to stick with better habits.

Being strict with yourself is not just about denying yourself the habits that have provided relief before. It is about finding ways to resolve the underlying bad feelings or anxiety so that they can replace the old habits. It is about finding new ways for quieting your stress response so that you are better able to control your impulses. Every time your stress response gets overactive, which is the case when you feel overwhelmed, lacking, or anxious, you have less access to the executive function of your brain, hence less control over your impulses.

Research has found that high amounts of stress are connected with low dopamine in the body. Low dopamine release means that you are more likely to be impulsive. This means that whenever you feel badly, the neural mechanisms in your brain kick in and you are driven to seek reward or pleasure to find relief. In contrast, when the stress response gets quieted, like is the case when you feel loved or when you deal with a problem adequately, your adrenaline levels fall and you can use more of your executive and cognitive brain functions. These functions include your ability to plan, problem solve, resist temptation, make better choices, and persist despite the challenges.

As you can see, the key is not about denying yourself, which would just make your brain feel like you are getting forced into a 'not enough' mode. It leaves you feeling worse and triggers you to keep seeking reward, which does not work. Being strict with yourself has to be rooted in loving yourself and committing to creating new habits that help you improve yourself and reach your goals. It is a positive effort. It is not a negativity or a denial. So how do you do it?

HOW TO BE STRICT WITH YOURSELF

- Think first and act later

When it comes down to it, resilience and mental fortitude are cemented by clear goals. That way, you know that there is a greater reward at stake. This knowledge empowers you to let go of instant gratification. Make a habit of thinking through every task you want to start. Prioritize it based on how you want to feel in the future. Do not just list the goal; think about the ways you will get there and then sort them by their importance within the context of your life. That way, when you have an impulse, you can always remember your long-term goal and control your response.

- Be an agent in your life

In the face of adversity, it is tempting to think that life happens to you. Anxiety kicks in because you start to imagine that you have no control over the circumstances of your life or that somehow, you are not strong enough to deal with your challenges. The antidote to this is to change your mindset to regain your power. When you are an agent in your life, you experience less fear because you are able to control your stress response. You are also able to tap into your inner drive and motivate yourself to act.

- Choose love

The love hormone, oxytocin, has been known to lower activation of the neural circuitry that causes anxiety. It also stimulates the brain's reward system. You can use the physiology of love in different ways to help you respond better to challenges. Practically, it means that you don't 'should' yourself or criticize yourself for not doing things as you believed you should. That is why the next section of this chapter is paramount.

The Stoics were big on self-governance. Rather than zoom in on other people's choices, they em-

THE POWER OF STOICISM

phasized on the individual and their morality. Stoicism is a personal philosophy meant to direct how you act, and no other Stoic emphasized the idea of being strict with yourself like Marcus Aurelius. He maintained that other people may be jerks or unreliable or fools. That is okay. They are allowed to choose who to be because that is their business. Your business is to choose discipline in your reactions and with yourself. If someone behaves in a ridiculous way, that is up to them. If you behave ridiculously, then you need to identify the problem, take a break, and work on preventing recurrence. The things you do are your business. Be strict about those and leave other people to themselves.

STRICTNESS IS NOT TYRANNY

It is worth noting that strictness is not synonymous with tyranny. The satisfaction you experience from yourself and the things you do is closely tied to the degree you tyrannize yourself. By definition, a tyrant is a cruel and oppressive leader. When you tyrannize yourself, you act toward yourself in an unloving way in the name of self-governance. It may work for a moment, but it is unsustainable. As it turns out, there are many tyrannies stemming from the many shoulds, hows, and whys you have come to believe. When you were young, you were malleable. You could absorb huge bits of information and interact with them as a sponge does with water. As you grew older, you started internalizing some of the behaviors and messages from people around you.

With time, as these messages start to cement themselves, you accept them as dogmas and rules and you start abiding by them. They may have been well thought out at the time they were learned. They may even have been well-intentioned, but if you take them on and follow them mindlessly, they become a tyrant. They take on a hostile, spiteful, and aimless shade and start torturing your sense of well-being. They stand in your way when you are trying to move forward as an adult and get your needs met. In many ways, they become a point of reference for your inner tyrant.

These personal tyrannies can take on different looks. They can be limiting beliefs, ideas, shoulds, and oughts that stress you and cause unnecessary tension. They separate you from reality and isolate you from other people. Here, I will discuss some that get in the way of persevering in the face of challenges. Becoming aware of them will help you to eliminate them. The key to fighting them is not to get angry that they exist. It is to recognize where they started, how they affect you, and then negotiate with yourself like you would someone you care about. The more you do this, the less power these tyrannies have over you. As you read them, analyze and accept them. When you face them, they will start melting away.

- The tyranny of urgency

Today's world is fast-paced and everything seems urgent. We chase abstract things fueled by unarticulated needs and desires. We are afraid that we will miss out or fail to rise up the career ladder fast enough, or be passed over for a promotion. The tyranny of urgency subjects you to tasks and external expectations which are always more urgent than the things you truly want to do. They end up increasing your stress and anxiety, causing you to give up on your true goals. To escape this tyranny, you need to slow down and step back. Get in the habit of constantly evaluating what matters to you.

As you evaluate what matters to you, shift your focus onto the process rather than the results. Disengage from the outcome and pay attention to the activity. Rather than obsess over when your next promotion will be, think about what you are doing to make it more likely to happen. While at it, favor quality over quantity. This is true for the things you are doing and the relationships you keep. The more rewarding something is, the more likely you are to stick with it when it becomes difficult. Rather than go about life doing only what feels urgent, you will learn to take your time and use it on what is purposeful and rewarding.

- The tyranny of should

From birth to death, we get bombarded with dogmas and messages - from culture, family, and media - which form obligations, making us think our needs will only be met if we behave in a certain way. This translates to the constant need to live up to different expectations that are sometimes beyond what you believe and who you are. These expectations seem to grow as you take on more influence and responsibility and they put a lot of pressure on you. The tyranny of should can steal from your energy and time.

While we cannot avoid some of the shoulds, we can interpret them in a way that frees us. Some of these shoulds exist so that our society can function with order. They strengthen intersocial bonds and maintain a peaceful co-existence. However, others are outdated and will manipulate your relationships rather than foster growth. Distinguishing which shoulds are helping you and which ones are toxic is not easy. You have to understand your needs and the different dynamics within the society. Ultimately, the antidote is self-awareness. As you become more well oriented, with a clear mental compass, then you can let go of the shoulds that drain you.

PRACTICE INTERNAL NEGOTIATION

As mentioned earlier, the way to deal with these tyrannies is to negotiate with yourself. Call your internal tyrant to a meeting and ask them what they fear would happen if you did not abide. Don't do this sarcastically or condescendingly. Be respectful and listen to your tyrant part. Most likely, it is a part of you that believes it is trying to protect you. Once you figure out what the fear is, negotiate with it. Would it give you some space if you addressed that fear in a different way? You can highlight that if it continues torturing you, you will be less able to deal with the fear. Make a promise to address the driving fear and keep that promise.

The goal is to create a respectful relationship with the tyrant so that it will not tighten its hold on you when it is afraid. Instead, teach it to tell you its fears and respond when it does. If this is new to you, it probably sounds strange, but it is drawn from Carl Jung's work on the different subpersonalities we have and how they affect us. The tyrant part of you is a subpersonality. If you make friends with it, it will be more likely to work with you toward your goals as opposed to impeding them.

USE GAMIFICATION TO GROW HABITS

You can turn it into a game. Gamification is a popular practice in economics and behavioral science. It is the process of using gaming princi-ples, elements, and mechanics to engage users in non-game contexts. In business, you can use gamification in employee training and evaluation, recruitment, and organizational productivity. It is also used in customer loyalty programs or in physical activity. The point of gamification in the different contexts is to encourage people to engage with something especially if the tasks they have to do are not enjoyable.

An example of gamification is where a business asks you to complete a set of tasks to get redeemable points or a badge. In a community set up, gamification would include putting you in groups so that you can solve problems together, complete activities, and achieve an objective. It is also gamification when businesses use discounts, coupons, or gift cards to fuel your engagement.

Regardless of the context, the idea is that clever design can promote good habits. Gamification is a powerful tool to use to encourage yourself to keep doing something that you know will benefit you even though you do not necessarily enjoy it at the moment. It is an antidote to tyrannizing yourself. Essentially, you create a reward system for yourself if you achieve a task or an objective that you find difficult. It has two principles:

- First, make sure your internal reference

points are against yourself. The question you will always be asking yourself is – how am I doing against my own potential? The only thing that matters is that you do your best.

- Secondly, what reward will I give myself for doing my best today?

2

LEARN HOW TO FACE REALITY

"Take care of this moment. Immerse yourself in it. Respond to this person or that person, this challenge, this deed. Quit avoiding. Stop giving yourself needless trouble. It is time to really live; to fully inhabit the situation you happen to be in right now. You are not some disinterested bystander. Participate. Exert yourself." — **Epictetus**

To be resilient is to be able to bounce back from adversity. It is to be tough. Resilient people know that they can overcome even the toughest setbacks that life puts in their way and still accomplish what they set out to do. As leaders, they know that they have a responsibility to guide their followers through challenges and usher them to success. Before Nelson Mandela became South Africa's first democratically elected leader, he was imprisoned for about three decades for his involvement in anti-apartheid activism. Reverend Martin Luther King Jr. had to overcome violence from the FBI, the media, and the public to lead the civil rights movement. Oprah Winfrey led a small production team for a while through a landscape that at the time had no room for black women. She managed to create a multimedia empire, producing magazines and books, and eventually, owned her network.

What made Oprah Winfrey, Martin Luther, and Nelson Mandela so unique? What quality fueled their resilience amidst challenging circumstances until they prevailed? Part of the answer to these questions lies in their ability to face reality. Your situation may not be as extreme as theirs, but everyone who has been successful has gone through a similar arch – they had to rise in a time of adversity and they had to garner the strength to lead their followers through it. Thanks to advances in technology, we live in an unprecedented time. There are major paradigm shifts happening in every sector of the world. Many of them bring challenges that you will encounter in different shapes depending on your situation in life. Whether you work in a fast-paced hospital environment, lead a global business, or are transitioning to a career that you are better suited for, you need the ability to face reality.

In truth, as a society, we need people who will help us go through tough times – whose focus on the larger picture will be unwavering and who will have the ability to rally groups around a worthy cause while keeping calm in the face of unrelenting trouble. These leaders are people, like you, who learn to refine and tap into their potential with every challenge that they meet, however small. They are people committed to resilience training in every step into their leadership position. They have accepted that no situation will ever be as idyllic as they would like it to be. They come to a crisis with a clear mind knowing that the clearer they are about the problem, the more likely they will be to stick with it until they find the solution. An accepting outlook toward reality helps to release stress and frees up the emotional and mental energy you need to lead effectively.

WHEN REALITY IS UNBEARABLE - ERICA'S STORY

Here is a rather extreme example to illustrate the point. Erica is a 29-year-old woman I met on a flight from Los Angeles. She was 27 at the time and hers is a story that demonstrates the transformative power of facing reality. Among the first statements she told me when I struck a conversation with her was, 'I always used to say I am very good at bad luck.' Talk about an oxymoron. I don't know about you, but when someone begins a story like that, I want to hear it all. At 23, she was trying to find her place in the world. She was working as a server in a restaurant in California and had managed to get her first car and move out of her parents' house. She was living with her friends and enjoying every bit of her new life. She could finally support herself and have some money to have fun.

Then, her expertise at bad luck struck. First, her car was stolen about ten minutes after she got to work. She did not find out until after work. Her boss pitied her so much that he bought her a new car the same day. She went to pick it up after they agreed on how much he would be deducting from her paychecks for the car payment. On her way home, the brake started smoking and then got stuck. Of course, she called her boss and explained the problem. He sent his son to fix the problem. The next day at work, she got a call from the police. They had found her stolen car less than a day after she filed the report. She went to pick it up and found it in excellent condition. She drove it to work.

At this point in the story, I wanted to know what happened to Erica's new car. Apparently, she got it back from her boss' son that morning. 'Who ends up without a car today and has two cars the next day?' She asked. 'That's some very good bad luck, don't you think?' We went on about other things until the conversation brought us back to the car issue. A short while after the 'very good bad luck,' Erica got a call from her ex saying he had totaled his car. She decided to lend him the one that had been stolen. They had been on and off for about five years, so she felt she could vouch for his character. By this point, Erica thought she had just overcome the worst things in life.

A week later, she was on her way to see her ex with her friend Karen when he called her to say he would come over. 'I couldn't get mad because we weren't together,' she said. She went home to find that he was already there, with her roommate. At this point, Erica flipped out. According to her, there comes a point in life when you stop trying to make everyone happy and fixing everything. She got into an argument with her roommate. She left the house for a walk to clear her mind but ended up driving to a bar. At 10pm, trying to get back home, she crashed her car into a telephone pole because she was not just pissed at her ex and her roommate, she was drunk. She broke her pelvis, neck, collarbone, all her ribs, and had hemiplegia and RT spastic. She lost control of her right side.

When I asked her what she thought of the accident, she said it could have been worse. She could have died, lost all of her memories, or become a vegetable. I was interested to know what lessons she learnt from the accident but I didn't want to ask. Then she offered. 'I have learned so much about myself, but the biggest lesson has to be "never run from your problems." You are better off confronting your problems rather than replacing them with new ones.' Erica had to relearn how to walk and talk while dealing with a broken heart and grieving a lost friendship. At her most vulnerable and weak moment, she had to face what was now her reality, find herself, and gather the strength to become a stronger and better person.

RESPOND, DON'T REACT

Trouble has a way of making us want to react, but resilient people face the situation squarely and respond appropriately. The difference between responding and reacting is a vital one to bear in mind. Responding, by definition, is showing a favorable reaction while reacting is exerting a force or influence that is in opposition to the trouble or challenge. This difference plays out in relationships and interactions and affects daily life. A reaction can happen within seconds. Because it tends to be immediate, it often lacks deliberation or thought, which means that it will likely not be the optimal way to handle the situation.

The argument here is not that reactions are bad. They are expected and normal. The problem comes when the immediacy of that reaction causes interpersonal difficulties for you. Think about it – most of the times that you reacted, your reactions were emotionally charged and often laced with anger. When you react, you may end up saying things that you wish you could take back. This is not true about a response. A response is by nature the outcome of reflection and thoughtfulness. It calls to you to consider the factors relevant to the situation and to formulate and present your response well. You do not shoot responses from the hip. You offer them with care, respect for others, and tolerance for differences. Responding demands that you remember that you are better than escaping or denying reality. To respond, you have to face what is, as it is.

ACCEPT THE HARSH REALITY – DARIO'S STORY

Dario married Anya in 2019. One morning in 2020, he woke up with a sinking feeling in his stomach. He was scheduled to go visit his wife but somehow, he knew he was not going to make it, yet again. They had parted in March 2019 for what was supposed to be two weeks, but they had not been able to meet again since. A series of events had brought them to that tough situation. They married in Germany. As a foreign couple, they expected that the paperwork would not be fast to process but they did not anticipate how complex the situation would be. In March, Anya went to Moscow to try and speed up the process. It took so long the Covid-19 outbreak lockdowns caught up with them.

March 2020 found Dario alone in Munich and his wife in Russia. He had to hold on to faith. As Steve Jobs puts it; 'sometimes life will hit you in the head with a brick. Hold on to faith.' At that point, his reality was too difficult to face. He wanted to ignore it, but he knew he could not. He embraced the strength that comes from facing a harsh reality. According to him, time is a lot like a river that moves you forward with realities that demand a decision from you. You can't stop the river's movement and you cannot avoid those harsh realities. You can only approach them the best way possible.

When Dario learned of the lockdowns, he was anxious. He had gotten through the previous months in the hope that he would see his wife soon but there was no knowing whether that was true anymore. No one was traveling at the time. It felt like it was bad news after another, with the stock market crashing and the whole world struggling to deal with a pandemic. When I got in contact with Dario, I knew after hearing him out that the first thing he needed to do was face the pain. He was trying hard to keep a regular routine and ignore all the chaos inside and around him. It took a while, but he got there. You see, whenever you confront something painful, you create an opportunity to choose the healthy and painful truth, or hold on to the unhealthy, comfortable delusion.

By failing to accept an uncomfortable reality, you choose a comfortable delusion. You choose fear, but you also choose to miss the chance to get stronger. Facing the truth, on the other hand, is choosing a better version of yourself. It is choosing strength. Dario had to accept that it was tough for him to be away from his wife. He had to admit that it hurt him to be alone without knowing when that could be rectified. When he was able to feel and reflect on his pain, he started to make progress.

The next step was for him to unpack the exact difficulties he was dealing with and decide what he could do. He could not change what had happened, but he could work to become better. So, we went through his options and without my prompting, Dario decided to dedicate a chunk of his days to things he was passionate about. When I prompted him, he said he meditated on death. Knowing that he would eventually die allowed him to accept that he was already vulnerable. The current misery could be worse. The more he did things he loved, the more alive he felt, and the more he could endure his bleak situation.

From his story, I learnt that facing reality, as harsh as it is, frees you up to do what you can do in the situation and gives you strength to endure. On the other hand, ignoring it keeps you stuck. The pain and discomfort that comes from challenges is temporary. When you deal with it, you create space in your mind to explore the opportunities available to you that allow you to evolve. The situation may still be harsh, but it will keep you moving. It will help you see the next steps you are responsible for. As Sylvester Stallone puts it, 'life is not about giving the hardest hit. It is about taking hard hits and still moving forward.'

HOW TO FACE REALITY

In theory, facing reality sounds easy, but many people still choose their version of reality. Your version of reality could be based on denial, disappointment, regret, or even waiting for something better, whether it is retirement or a promotion. Failing to face reality is the reason people stay in an unfulfilling job position or stay in the wrong profession. It is the reason leaders keep under-performing employees in their team or keep applying the same techniques hoping for different results. There are few better things you can do for yourself than giving up on a fictional version of your reality. Even when your situation is difficult, you cannot improve it without acknowledging the way it is. Here are three ways to help you face a reality you don't like and determine how to change it into one you are proud of:

- **Admit your pretense**

Acceptance is about unconditionally valuing all the parts that make you who you are. It means acknowledging the good and the parts that need to be improved. It means admitting and dropping your pretenses. For many people, this is hard because they tend to self-criticize. If that is you, you need to look at your state of mind. Remember that facing reality may not be easy, but it will make you happier and will guarantee a better future. Understanding and accepting your reality is the basis for working with it. It is both purposeful and practical. It will help you choose your goals and how to achieve them. It will help you deal with challenges gracefully.

When you admit your own pretense, you can start creating a new future. Denying the current reality, more so if it is uncomfortable, does not make it any less so. Dealing with the discomfort is the way to get to the good stuff, but it will demand practice. The stoics taught that to fully accept your situation, you have to acknowledge any role you played, whether bad or good, in getting you there. You have to name your contribution toward failure or success. That way, you know what you are dealing with and you can determine your next best steps.

Bear in mind that you cannot fix what you do not acknowledge as a problem. When it comes to your negative contributions to a problem, think of them as opportunities to learn. Remind yourself that you can control your reality. You are the only one who can put in the necessary work to change it. The goal is to be able to accept all the parts of your reality, and not only the things that need work. Make sure you accept your successes and your strengths as well. It will empower you to see that you can do better when you need to.

- **Don't let fear control you**

Fear is a powerful tool if you know how to wield it, but it can be oppressive if you let it control you. This is especially true if you let your fear of what others think of you get in your way. You have to be willing to do things as uniquely as you think is best and then reflect on the feedback you get, without surrendering your perspectives. It is easy, especially in the face of adversity, to look in the mirror and identify all your insecurities. But facing your reality also includes counting your positives. List your strengths and everything you are good at. Detail your accomplishments and the work you put in to get there. Counting your competencies will improve your attitude and help you keep going when challenged. As a rule of thumb, pause and reflect when you find yourself thinking in terms of 'shoulds.' Don't get caught up living the life you think you are supposed to be living. Instead, work on making the reality you want.

- **Outsmart your biases**

Sometimes, the thing getting in the way of embracing your reality is not even conscious. We all have cognitive biases that make our judgments inaccurate because your brain chooses the bias over hard evidence. A cognitive bias makes your judgments consistently irrational. Research has found that such biases can force you to make unreasonable decisions. They can make you act in ways that are inconsistent with your beliefs, values, and reason. The way to outsmart these biases is to know them. Here are the most common biases that get in the way of facing your reality:

- The Dunning-Kruger effect – the belief that you are more skilled or smarter than you are. It prevents you from admitting to your weaknesses and limitations.
- Confirmation bias – this bias makes you favor the information that conforms to your existing beliefs. It makes you disregard anything that does not conform to your beliefs, even when it is accurate.
- Availability heuristic – this is a mental shortcut that leads you to believe that the first thing that comes to your mind is the right choice.
- Self-serving bias – in this case, you blame

external forces for the difficulties you are experiencing and credit yourself when things are going well.

- Attentional bias – attentional bias keeps your focus only on some things and allows you to ignore others.

3

BECOME COMFORTABLE
WITH FLEXIBILITY

'Make the best of what is in your power, and take the rest as it happens.' – **Epictetus**

I f you have ever woken up and found your body achy and stiff, you know why flexibility is important. Physically speaking, flexibility helps you move at your discretion without feeling like you have something on your back. It makes it easy for you to perform daily tasks that require fitness, varying degrees of stretching, and a range of motion without incurring injuries. It allows you to navigate life with a sense of ease. It is even more important if you are involved in heavy physical activity. Your body is constantly under stress from external factors, whether they be home-related activities or fitness. In short, being physically flexible has many benefits. It helps you to feel good in your body.

Physical flexibility is to the body what mental/psychological flexibility is to your mental well-being. We are constantly faced with moments and situations that challenge us and leave us experiencing many unwelcome feelings. We like to imagine that sheer willpower or logic can force us out of those situations, but it cannot. This is where psychological flexibility comes in. When we leverage it, we are able to see our problems for what they are and make our decisions more intentional. This holistic view allows us to endure in the face of adversity and to navigate it with more purpose and clarity, improving the quality of our life.

In 2020, The United States, among many other governments in the world, declared Covid-19 a national emergency. When that happened, the way people and businesses operated changed in unprecedented ways. It was a terrifying period, but leaders who had learnt to lean on flexibility were able to thrive, experiment, and pivot, proving the critical value of flexibility in fostering resilience. One example is when distillery owners stopped producing liquor and started producing sanitizer which was needed to keep the frontline workers safe. Other companies like Ford and GM pivoted and started producing ventilator machines instead of letting their facilities stay idle.

What was it that the leaders of these businesses had? They were not afraid to adapt. They looked at disruptions and challenges as opportunities instead of burdens. This is what allowed them to realize the potential their businesses had. This principle holds true for personal adversity. When you look at it as an opportunity, you can realize your personal potential and your capacity to change for the better. Whenever things change, you have an opportunity to make them better. Developing psychological flexibility has countless advantages in times of challenge. Research shows that flexibility can help you to reduce anxiety, stress, PTSD, depression, and other mental health issues.

Studies also show that flexibility helps to build resilience and can help people manage intense physical and emotional pain. If something is externally terrifying, threatening, or troubling, there are ways to get rid of it. You can remove it or you can avoid it in the future. The situation is different when it comes to our internal experiences. Trying to remove or avoid them is like trying to move a 1,500kg boulder alone. The more you try, the more tired you will become. This means that if you feel a lack of confidence at work, for example, if you are angry, anxious, afraid to fail, or overwhelmed, you will identify the feeling as the problem. Then, you will try to get rid of it because we believe that the feeling needs to go before we can enjoy our lives. Yet, the more you spend time trying to push these feelings away, the less energy you have for family, work, or anything else that matters to you. If you are psychologically flexible, you can assess the situation causing the emotion, not just the emotion. You can make choices that will leave you feeling more secure because they will align with your values. What then, is psychological flexibility?

WHAT IS MENTAL FLEXIBILITY?

Psychological flexibility includes the ability to stay present in the moment. It involves staying open to experiencing the different feelings and thoughts which show up, whether they are good or bad, and then taking action that serves your values. It is a core concept used by psychologists in Acceptance and Commitment Therapy (ACT). ACT was first developed by a clinical psychologist and professor, Steven Hayes. According to him, the practice is an evidence-based practice that uses acceptance, mindfulness, and methods based on the patient's values. It teaches strategies to keep you conscious and present so that you choose a response that is well aligned with your goals and values.

Psychological flexibility is integrally tied to emotional regulation. It is about giving yourself a way to take conscious actions even when you are in distress. A psychologically flexible person is able to make choices that are based on their values and their beliefs rather than the emotions that they are feeling in the moment. They experience reduced depression and anxiety, a stronger connection with their loved ones, and increased emotional resilience as a result. In contrast, a psychologically inflexible person can be noted by the actions they take in response to adversity no matter how well those actions align with their values. For example, if you are inflexible, you will cope with stress by avoiding it. You will be overwhelmed by worry and anxiety when faced with challenges, you will lose your vision for your future, and you will be unable to recognize any unhelpful patterns in your behavior. A psychologically flexible person will be able to demonstrate the following:

- Intellectual flexibility – when they go into any situation, they walk in with an open mind. They are able to take in new information, integrate it, and draw conclusions from it. They do not struggle when switching between the big picture and the details that constitute the big picture.
- Creativity – flexibility is closely tied to actively looking for new ways to solve problems and tackle challenges. It is having the courage and confidence to experiment or improvise.
- Receptiveness – a mentally flexible person is receptive to change. They are able to respond to it with a positive attitude. They are always willing to learn new ways to achieve objectives and targets.
- Behavior modification – mental

flexibility is incomplete if it does not factor in a change in behavior. Of what use is accepting change if you do not adjust your actions to accommodate it? A mentally flexible person is able to adjust their style of working or their approach to meet the needs of an emergency or a situation.

There are people who are naturally adaptable. They seem to thrive when the unexpected happens. They flourish when their routines have to change. However, this is not most people. The majority of us have to take a moment to adjust when our 'to do' list is disrupted. The good news, though, is that you can learn to be flexible. You may even have an advantage over people who are naturally adaptable. Because you have honed your organizing and planning skills, you can rely on them to help you make the necessary pivot in the face of adversity.

THE PSYCHOLOGICAL FLEXIBILITY MODEL

To understand flexibility even better, let us consider how one school of thought breaks it down.

According to the Association for Contextual Behavioral Science, to develop flexibility, you have to develop six major processes described in the next section. As a rule of thumb, deal with each one of them at a time and progress through them all. Do not feel the need to attack all of them at once.

- Live in the present moment

When you are faced with a situation that you find challenging, notice the challenges. Go inward and observe the ways you struggle with feelings and thoughts that do not serve you well. Rather than getting unconsciously wrapped up in a war to get rid of them or to avoid them, see if you can gently stop the cycle. Do so by identifying the feelings and thoughts and sitting with them.

- Accept your thoughts

We all have a common desire to get rid of the parts in us that we do not like or that we are ashamed of. Suppressing these aspects takes more work, damages your psychological wellbeing, and erodes resilience. Hiding them is counter-productive to changing your behavior. According to the ACT model, embrace these feelings or thoughts and use the energy you save to control your behavior instead of your thoughts.

- Stay true to your values

When you are faced with adversity, your values may not be very clear. If that is the case, take time to remind yourself of what is important to you in the long run. Remember that your values are not the same as your goals. For example, your goal may be to run a marathon, and the value under-pinning it would be to prioritize your health. Not working during the weekend could be a long-term goal, but your value may be spending time with your family. Whatever the case, make sure you stay true to your values.

- Cognitive defusion

This principle is about separating your thoughts from who you are. Language is powerful and how you use it to label your feelings and yourself cor-relates with your view of yourself. How do you interpret your feelings and your thoughts? Are you troubled by the feeling, the actual thought, or the meaning/interpretation you assign to the thought? This is a deeply stoic idea. It is incredible how fast you can move from engaging a painful thought such as 'I made a mess of that assignment,' to 'I am such a failure,' and then to panicking that your career is over and you are close to being homeless. With cognitive defusion, you separate the labels or negative language interpreting your feelings from who you are. By practicing awareness of how you are using language and changing it, you create space between your feelings and how you react.

- Use the self as context

This is one of the difficult aspects of the ACT model. It relates to mindfulness. It involves the ability to see yourself as separate and to separate who you are from where you have been and how you judge yourself. True, your past contributes to who you are, but there is more to you than your experiences. Use the self as context when you are tempted to label yourself in response to adversity instead of dealing with it. Here, you are called upon to notice that you are hosting a thought, but the thought is not rooted in any other truth besides your thoughts. From there, you reframe the thought and remind yourself that that is all it is –

a thought. It is not the absolute truth. You can go a step further and remind yourself how varying your thoughts are by the moment, hour, or day. The idea is to eventually treat your feelings and thoughts as passing weather systems rather than a reflection of yourself. The separation distances you from changing emotions and negative thoughts. It allows you to step back and assess your challenges from a neutral position.

- Take action committed to your values

The final process according to the flexibility model is taking committed action. It is about acting in alignment with your values. When you are faced with a choice to change course or to pivot, ask yourself, 'what do I need to do to align my actions with my values? What can I do at the moment to honor my values instead of reacting to my feelings?' By asking these questions, you make space to choose how you respond. You give yourself the power and the freedom to endure difficult circumstances.

Bear in mind that developing psychological flexibility does not translate to a pain-free life. Emotional discomfort is very much a part of life, and that is okay. It does mean, however, that you will not be adding suffering by struggling against your experiences. It means that more often than not, you will live in alignment with what you believe. Remember that flexibility alone does not guarantee that you reach all your goals, but it guarantees that you will be in more control of your response, and you will give yourself your best shot at reaching your goals no matter what comes against you.

TESTING YOUR MENTAL FLEXIBILITY

So, you have read this chapter and you are wondering where you are when it comes to mental flexibility. There are a number of approaches psychologists use to test mental flexibility. Here, you will find two approaches that you can use to determine where you rank and how you can start working on your mental flexibility:

- **The STAR technique**

If you have ever gone for a job interview, you know that you will not be given the job for simply stating that 'I am quick on my feet,' or 'I can adapt to situations.' Any interviewer worth

their salt will need you to prove that you can actually be flexible by giving appropriate examples.
The STAR technique helps you to find examples
where you have demonstrated flexibility or
where you could have done better by drawing on
situations like moving to a new country for work,
working with people of a different culture, balancing part-time work and study, or living
abroad on an exchange program. The experience
could be any one you choose. Take a piece of
paper and write down a situation where you had
to adapt to change or where you needed to be
flexible. Describe it using the STAR technique.

S - Define the Situation (*Where were you? What
were you doing? What was the context?*)

T – Find the Task (*What was your goal? What was
the problem?*)

A – Detail the Action (*Clearly state what you did*)

R – Detail the Result (*What outcome did your action
produce?*)

Here is an example of what it might look like:

Situation: I initially applied for a promotion at
work that was contingent upon passing an exam.
I acted on my friends' advice. I knew that I would

do well in some aspects of the test, but I wasn't sure I was ready for others. I got a response that the job would be mine if I passed. However, I didn't do as well as I hoped.

Task: I had to rethink my future and I had to do it fast. I could wait and re-apply for the same promotion in three years, or I could request to retake the test at a sooner date, study as hard as I could, and then hopefully do better this time. Whatever my choice, I had to be flexible because each choice had serious implications.

Action: I decided that even though the promotion was important to me, what was more important was that I actually learn my job and become more competent at what I do. After getting more information about the test and the company's promotion policies, I decided to take my time before re-taking the test. I enrolled in evening classes to help me strengthen my weak spots and I enlisted the help of a colleague to practice.

Result: At first, I was very upset that I had to change my plans, but I was later pleased that I did. I am convinced that I made the right decision. Five months later, I had the opportunity to retake the test and I aced it this time. I was promoted and recommended to the board as an upcoming talent to watch. That was two and half years earlier than I expected I would be promoted.

The person in this example had a choice to make. Despite their feelings, they chose an action aligned with their values, which helped them become more flexible and persevere in a difficult situation (not getting the promotion they wanted). The result was positive. To use this technique well, remember that you are the STAR in the story. Focus on the actions you made no matter how big or small they were. Make sure you tell a story, but do not add unnecessary details. The idea is for you to see how well you were able to transition in the face of disruptions or challenges.

- **The Acceptance and Action Questionnaire (AAQ)**

You can also use the AAQ to help you rate your behavior and determine your flexibility levels. The questionnaire rates behavior on a scale. You add up the scores to get your total score. The higher your score is, the less psychologically flexible you are. Note that you are meant to repeat these questions across time and compare your results. Compare your previous results as you grow, not another person's score. This way, you are able to track how you are changing with time. Do not try to get a perfect score. Instead, concentrate on getting better over time. Below is a list of the seven statements in the AAQ. Rate each of them on a scale of 1 to 7, as follows:

1 - Never true

2 - Very seldom true

3 - Seldom true

4 - Sometimes true

5 - Frequently true

6 - Almost always true

7 - Always true

- My painful memories and experiences make it hard for me to live a life that I would care for.
- I fear my feelings.
- I worry that I will not be able to control my feelings.
- Emotions mess up my life.

- My memories are painful. They prevent my life from being fulfilling.
- Worry gets in the way of my success.
- It looks like most people are doing life better than me.

4

ACCEPT SUFFERING AS PART OF LIFE

'How does it help to make troubles heavier by bemoaning them?' - **Seneca.**

R esilient people understand that shit happens. They have accepted the fact that suffering is as much a part of life as is happiness. This does not mean that they welcome suffering or that they are delusional. It means that when tough times come, they understand that pain is part of human existence. Knowing this stops you from feeling discriminated against when you meet adversity. Never once do they find themselves wondering why they had to suffer. They never ask 'why me?' In fact, resilient people seem to automatically re-

378

spond to adversity with a question of their own - 'why not me?' They know that terrible things happen to them just like they do to everyone else.

During troubling times, resilient people are able to accept that their life has changed, and the difficult life is their cup in that moment. They know that the real question is whether or not they will swim or sink. We live in an age where not enough people seem to know that 'man is born unto trouble.' We imagine that we are entitled to an Instagram perfect life. Yet, the truth of the matter is, suffering comes for us all.

SUFFERING BUILDS RESILIENCE

Throughout history, human beings have wondered whether suffering matters and what role it plays in life. It is our universal nature to pursue pleasure and to run away from pain. Culture dances to this tune and informs the way we deal with suffering. In western culture, we seem averse to suffering. The default is to look at it as an unwelcome interruption in the pursuit of happiness. When pain comes, we repress it, fight it, search for easy solutions to get rid of it, and when all else fails, we medicate it. Some cultures, more so in the East, have a different view of suffering. They acknowledge the role it plays in the lives of people in the path toward enlightenment.

We can argue whether or not it is possible to be fully enlightened or reach nirvana – a state of permanent and perfect inner peace – but there is plenty we can learn from how Buddhists approach life's disappointments, defeats, and imperfections. According to Buddhist philosophy, suffering has four major benefits – it produces compassion, a respect for reality, wisdom, and resilience. We come out of suffering wiser than when we got in. When things are going well, we rarely stop to question life and its meaning. It is difficult situations that force us out of a mindless state and allow us to reflect on how we go through life. So as to see deeply and to create in ourselves what the Christians call a wise heart, we have to pass through the eye of the storm.

Nietzsche, a man of inarguable wisdom, is said to have remarked that anything that does not kill us will leave us stronger. Suffering builds resilience. It leaves us better able to endure hardship. The same way your muscles get stronger when you endure the pain of exercise, is the same way we have to endure some emotional pain so as to strengthen our emotional muscles. Hellen Keller, a woman who knew more than her share of suffering and joy in her lifetime, said that you cannot develop character in quiet and ease. It is only the experience of suffering and trial that strengthens the soul, inspires ambition, clears vision, and births success.

Secondly, everyone hurts, and allowing ourselves to be part of this universal reality links us together and creates compassion for one another. According to the Oxford dictionary, compassion is an awareness of the suffering of others coupled with a wish to see them relieved of it. The only way to gain that awareness of others' suffering is to have suffered. It is not enough to understand suffering theoretically. An academic description is useless; it is like describing color to a blind person. To really know pain, you have to experience it. According to the stoics, suffering and joy, if we allow them, teach us how to show empathy. They transport us into the heart and soul of another person. In those moments of vulnerability, we get to know other people's sorrows and joys and we get to care as if those concerns were our own.

Thirdly, suffering inevitably creates a deep respect for reality. The experiences of joy and happiness connect us to what is infinitely possible, but experiencing pain reminds us of our finitude. It gets us deeply acquainted with our limitations. When, despite whatever we try, we still get hurt, we are humbled by our humanity, which we often miss when things are going well. No wonder when we are happy and prospering, we look to the heavens and when we are in pain, we cast down our gaze to the finite. It has been suggested that we need to always carry around two pieces of paper. The first one needs to state that 'the world was made for me' and the second one, 'I am but a man.' A healthy and resilient mind lives somewhere between these two truths. It is suspended somewhere between humility and hubris. In the same way balancing those truths creates better psychological health, experiencing both joy and pain creates a healthy relationship with reality.

Joy and ecstasy make us feel invincible. They lead us to believe that we are the masters of our destiny and that we create our destinies, but pain makes us feel humbled and vulnerable. It leads us to believe that we are servants to our circumstances. It shows us how limited our control over reality is. If you experience only joy and good times, you become arrogant. If you experience only suffering, you resign to life. The ups and downs of life bring us close to what Aristotle called the golden mean. They give us a respect for reality that accepts our limitations, humanity, and our potential. Understanding that suffering is inevitable and that it could be beneficial helps us to become more accepting when it befalls us. And when we are able to accept sorrow and grief as necessary, we suffer less.

Nathaniel Branden, a Canadian psychotherapist, links the issue of suffering to self-esteem – which demands self-acceptance. He defines it as the white blood cells of consciousness. Healthy white blood cells do not mean that you will not get sick. They mean that you get sick less often and that even then, you will recover faster. Similarly, suffering will not go away because you have accepted its inevitability, but you will have a stronger consciousness; which means that you will suffer less often and when you do, your recovery will be faster. The fact that suffering can be beneficial does not imply that you look for opportunities for it. By nature, we seek pleasure and we try to minimize pain. The impermanent and imperfect world provides enough opportunities for adversity without us having to look for them so that we can become more resilient. Yet, we cannot deny that learning to accept and even embrace the inevitability of pain allows it to become an instrument and a tool for growth.

REASONS YOU STRUGGLE TO ACCEPT SUFFERING

Say you are going through a breakup or a divorce and are struggling to move on. Maybe you were passed over for a promotion that you know you deserved. Perhaps you lost a loved one or experienced a traumatic event that you had no control over. Maybe the challenges you are facing have nothing to do with you in the present and everything to do with parental neglect as a child. Perhaps you feel stuck and are having trouble moving on, or even articulating your emotions. There are all kinds of situations that present as a challenge to overcome, some of them internal and others external. You can know all the theories about how beneficial suffering can be and still struggle to accept that it will come. If that is you, what is the problem?

For some people, the struggle to accept adversity comes from a misunderstanding. They imagine that acceptance is the same as agreeing with what happened or making it permissible. For others, the denial is more about fear of dealing with the pain that comes with acceptance. Whatever your reason, lack of acceptance is normal and to some extent, common, but it is not necessarily beneficial. You can learn and influence yourself to feel differently and eventually get to acceptance. It will just demand dedication and practice.

The problem with failing to accept the inevitability of suffering is that whenever you try to numb pain, you are also choosing to shun happiness and joy. Avoiding your emotions creates more problems for you in the long run, including addiction, anxiety, and depression. Calm acceptance allows you to deal with your emotions and keep going. It is normal to react to challenges and negative situations with emotions like anger, blaming yourself or others, sadness, or regret, but you can tell whether you are struggling with acceptance if you find yourself experiencing more than seven of the following thought patterns:

- This is unfair.

- I cannot deal with this.
- Why am I going through this?
- Things should not be this way.
- I should not have to deal with this.
- I cannot believe I am going through this.
- Why am I going through this now?
- This is not right.
- Why me?
- The universe has conspired against me.
- I really don't deserve this.
- I will never feel okay about this.
- No one else has to go through this stuff.
- I never get a break.
- I cannot get over this.
- I always attract bad things.

SUFFERING CAN CREATE PURPOSE AND MEANING

Understandably, when you are in the thick of things, you wonder whether suffering has any point to it. Does it give meaning to life? Many religions see some utility in suffering. For Christians, suffering brings them closer to God. It wakes them up when they are getting too complacent in their happiness. As one author put it, 'God whispers in our pleasure but shouts in our pain. Pain is his way of rousing a deaf world. It removes any pretenses and plants truth in a rebel soul.' Of course, some people take this idea to extremes. One dentist remarked that life would be better without anesthesia because 'men would endure what God meant for them to endure.'

Modern-day psychologists may not go as far as the Christians and certainly not as the dentist, but they agree that you can get many benefits from terrible experiences. Everyone has heard of PTSD. The alternative, when someone deals with the trauma, is post-traumatic growth. According to Richard Tedeschi, people understand themselves better, they know their world better, and they relate with others better when they have suffered. They live life better.

There is reason to be skeptical about the psychological process that leaves you better after adversity. For starters, most studies in the field have looked into people's perception of their reaction to trauma and not their actual reactions. Researchers have not considered actual and concrete changes in people's lives and psyches in response to trauma. It does not help matters that some research suggests that the same changes that happen after trauma can also happen after a major positive life event. It could be real growth or a perception of growth. Still, these are just minor objections to an overwhelming body of research. George Bonanno talks about our ability to endure trauma. According to him, we are born to grow in resilience.

The news gets better. We become antifragile – the resilient person resists shock and they become better. In one study, respondents were given a list with over 30 negative life events including the death of a loved one, physical assault, and so forth. They were instructed to tick whichever one they had experienced in their lives. Those who reported never having gone through such events were found to have lower than average pain tolerance. They also were more likely to catastrophize stressful situations. The group of people who experienced most of the negative experiences also had the same pattern. The difference was in the group who had an average number of bad experiences. They were found to be kinder, calmer under stress, and had a high pain tolerance.

The research also found that suffering and meaning are inevitably connected. People who describe their lives as meaningful tend to report more struggle than those who describe their lives as happy. Countries whose citizens report more meaning are often the poor ones. Conversely, countries with the happiest people are safe and prosperous. In the same way, the jobs people find most meaningful like working in the medical field or as a clergy involve handling people's pain. For a moment, think about the most meaningful experiences in your life. What do you notice about them? These experiences tend to be either very painful or very pleasant. What is more, we tend to choose pursuits that will test us – whether it is raising children or training for a marathon. We do these things because we know that these pursuits matter.

Needless to say, there is a huge difference between the struggles we choose – our hobbies, careers, children, etc., and the suffering that is unwelcome and unchosen. Undoubtedly, the suffering we choose affords us opportunity for personal growth, meaning, and pleasure. It is with the unchosen suffering that the questions roll in. The truth is, any suffering can spark change if we let it. It can liberate us and help us pursue more meaningful pursuits. There is no getting around it. Would it be better if we never suffered?

Maybe. But are there things in suffering we can take solace in? Absolutely. When you accept the inevitability of suffering, it will not just scar you. It will give your life meaning and purpose.

NOTICE THE SMALL PURPLE FLOWERS

A couple of years ago, a friend of mine, someone who had been very committed to social justice activism and self-awareness, said these words to me: 'I feel guilty all the time for how much suffering there is in the world and how little I can do about it. I can't even let myself enjoy a banana knowing the conditions in which it was harvested.' We make personal and ethical choices all the time, but when my friend said these words to me, she was deeply depressed. She was not saying that she was depressed because she had sacrificed eating bananas, or that it was the depression that stopped her from eating a banana. She was saying that she had a tendency to push pleasure away. She sensed that she was more open to suffering than she was to joy. She also sensed that she was exhausted by that reality.

By and large, western culture is suffering-phobic. We learn from an early age to shun pain, fear, and shame. We are taught to shy from the suffering of others as if, somehow, their suffering will taint us if we get too close. We grow up believing that we are better off if we tuck away and hide suffering. For the sake of resilience, we need to learn to associate suffering with compassion rather than disdain and like my friend, we also need to accept and absorb pleasure. If we cannot do this, we will burn out. There is so much happening around and within us. Trying to be fully awake to its demands for perspective, balance, and energy means that we stop getting attached to results. It means that in all the bad news, we also notice the good news and stay open to it.

In the winter of 2015, I was in Maui on a retreat with some of my close friends. I found myself ashamed whenever I told anyone else where I was going. The weather there was amazing, but when friends asked how my trip was going, I would tell them how humid it was, implying that things were not as I had expected. I was disowning the intense pleasure of the experience. I spent a lot of time there preventing myself from experiencing pleasure and instead indulged in self-deprecation and guilt. Maybe I thought that distancing myself from pleasure would protect others from feelings of jealousy. Or perhaps I felt that I was abandoning my friends who were enduring the winter if I enjoyed my trip. Or maybe I was just struggling to let joy in and admit that it is okay to enjoy the small purple flowers in Maui. I deserved to be as happy as everyone else.

At the time, I was not very conscious of what was happening, but it is quite common if you think about it. How often do you get a compliment and your automatic response is 'No, no …!'? We have a way of distorting our experiences through mental habits. In meditation, there is a practice to get around these patterns of distortion but you have to be aware of how they play out. When you notice a feeling like anger rising because of discomfort or pain, for example, rather than noticing it, you start to blame yourself or wonder for how long you will be angry. These responses distract you from the feeling and distort how you relate with it.

As Buddha would put it, true and real happiness is an arm of resilience. It is not about feeling as if everything is great. It is about recognizing that you have the inner resources and are connected to others, which keeps you from getting depleted by tough experiences and emotions. Accepting the inevitability of suffering does not mean that you ignore the small purple flowers by the roadside. It means you notice them and perhaps, if you can, stop and smell them. It means that you learn to take in joy and be nourished by it and you learn to take in pain and be shaped by it. Happiness and growth are available in pain and joy. Please help yourself.

5

LEAD WITH A QUIET MIND

'Don't explain your philosophy. Embody it.'
– Epictetus.

M ost of the time, when we think of a great leader, we imagine someone who is excellent at multitasking, quickly sifting through crazy amounts of data, articles, and emails with unbridled enthusiasm. Nothing could be further from the reality. An excellent leader leads with a quiet mind. They remain peaceful and calm, ready to deal with any business challenges that come their way. Of course, this is not as easy in practice as it is in speech. Today's culture is one of information overload. There are distractions everywhere, but this chapter deals with the distractions lurking within your mind, stealing your attention, and reducing your performance, slowly killing your ability to focus. Without being aware of it, the distraction is robbing you of the ability to endure adversity.

I am not talking about the distraction of messages, emails, technology, people dropping by your office, or other notifications. After many years of working with different professionals, I can say with certainty that the biggest obstacle in the path of a quiet mind is the mind in survival mode. It is a mind with unchecked mental chatter, doubts, concerns, and unwanted worries that draw your focus away from the problems at hand. The true leader's mind is quiet and free of these distractions.

A quiet mind has been celebrated and revered by the greatest thinkers in history and in our time. These people intuitively made leaps that changed the course of history. In a world of ever-increasing information, frenetic energy, and urgency, there is a need to return to the old emphasis of leading from a quiet mind. You cannot effectively lead or exert influence on others if you are unable to lead your own life. It is simply impossible. For starters, a quiet mind has been linked to good decision making, which is necessary for good leadership.

Ultimately, the success of the projects you start and the teams you lead rests on the quality of your choices. Your choices can only be as sound as the processes and inputs you use to reach them. Neuro-science and behavioral science have proven that our brains are struggling with emotional overload. According to research, we receive more than 11 million data inputs and stimuli per second and we can only consciously process 40. When we multitask, the amount of data we can process decreases even further.

Daniel Kahneman, a Nobel Prize-winning economist, describes it like this: 'Our brains have evolved to make most decision-making automatic and reliant upon biases and shortcuts. This works well if you are in the wild, needing instinct to tell you whether to run away from a rustling leaf or the shadow of a predator, but it is not suitable for the modern workplace.' Research shows that we get more biased when we are working in teams, under social and personal pressure to self-silence or conform to the group. The resilient leader learns to overcome these obstacles so that they can get the best out of their teams and themselves. Fortunately, behavioral sciences have designed ways to outsmart our brains, but before we dig into those, let's look at how our mindsets affect our teams.

HOW YOUR MINDSET AFFECTS YOUR TEAM

In 2017, a research team in Harvard University surveyed people to understand their typical work day. They collected more than 2000 responses and learnt that 80% of the respondents experienced annoyance, stress, or monotony. They also reported engaging in escapist activities like watching TV, drinking, or other online distractions. The most illuminating thing about the responses is the mindset behind them. It turns out that by nature, our minds produce emotional and thought patterns that make our life experiences negative. We have evolved this way as part of the drive to survive. We are programmed to see the worst possible scenarios and the emotions produced are geared towards self-preservation. For instance, if I am unsure whether what I am looking at is a snake or a stick, my mind will assume that it is a snake so that I run and save my life.

The problem with this way of thinking is that if you show up at home or at work feeling that life is annoying or stressful and something you have to escape from, you will not lead as best as you could. Fortunately, there is good news. Your mind can be trained to look at situations and respond to the automatic emotions and thoughts your brain produces differently. That way, you experience every day from a grounded and positive perspective. You still notice the negative emotions that were meant to help you survive, but they do not control you. Such training allows you to respond to challenges better, increase your focus, improve your resilience, and create a productive and enjoyable life.

How your mindset affects your leadership may not be straightforward. You may imagine that your emotional patterns and automatic thoughts affect only you, but that is far from the truth. Improving your internal perceptions can improve your external experiences. When your mind is oriented towards connection, creativity, and contribution, you can authentically strengthen work and personal relationships.

After all, life and business are filled with obstacles and decisions that include others. On the other hand, when your mind is creating repetitive drama around daily natural circumstances, you are wasting a lot of energy. That internal drama prevents you from connecting better and making better choices. Mental training can help you switch your focus from the negative to the real.

INFLUENCING OTHERS WITH A QUIET MIND

I like to give examples using professional athletes because I see a connection between leaders and athletes. Both of them have to consistently produce results in a critical, transparent, and highly competitive world with many factors out of their control. Since top performers are often excelling in their field, they are sometimes unaware of how poorly they are experiencing life. It is easy to confuse financial success and achievement with having a life you enjoy. Leaders both in business and sports have to deal with the same challenges to productivity – struggling to be in the moment and to listen, and being hyper critical of themselves. You cannot improve these things with sheer willpower. You have to capture and train your mind.

Our world is constantly changing and there is an ever-growing complexity. There is also more noise and distraction. The more complex your external environment becomes, the more you need your mind to be right. The more noise there is around you, the quieter your mind needs to be. Effective leadership starts when you begin managing your internal behaviors so that you are more present, connected, and authentic in a very complex environment. This whole process must begin from acknowledging that the survival mind is an enemy.

The unwanted noise in your head lamenting, judging, forecasting, imagining, and assessing without your permission is not your friend. The uninvited negative self appraisals are a survival trait that remained in your mind after many years of evolution. They are not you. You have to dethrone them as your advisor. Begin noticing that you do not think thoughts on purpose. One feature of the survival mind is that it is automatic. If you trust its advice, it gets stronger and makes it harder for you to focus and endure adversity.

WHY GROWTH STARTS IN YOUR MIND

If you want to improve your resilience and leadership, you cannot ignore your mind. In 2016, a team of researchers from California took two years to study the strategies that create great leadership. They interviewed more than 250 executives from McKinsey, Microsoft, LEGO, Google, and other C-suite companies, and assessed over 35,000 leaders. They compared their findings with the available research studies on leadership and they found that across board, leadership starts with yourself. It begins in the mind.

In understanding the way your mind works, you are able to lead yourself well. If you can lead yourself effectively, you can understand and trust others, which will help you to lead them better. 'Better' and 'effectively' in this context means that you are able to tap into your sense of purpose and intrinsic motivations, and other people's, so that you can endure difficulties. Anyone who is able to do that can persist. They become more engaged and more productive in their work and more importantly, they create stronger human connectedness, happiness, and better relation-ships even beyond their area of influence.

As it turns out, there are many concrete and mea-surable benefits from being engaged as a leader and inspiring the same in your people. There is a hospitality company headquartered in Maryland, Marriott International, that stands out because of its focus on other people. The founders have one overarching philosophy for business: 'if we care for our people, they will care for our guests and business will iron itself out.' Currently, they have over 700,000 employees all over the world but they still keep their commitment to caring for their employees. Their approach seems effective too. A recent internal survey of their team showed that more than 83% of the employees find their leaders relevant and engaging. For con-text, only 13% of workers across different indus-tries in the US feel engaged in their work.

When it comes to quieting your mind, there are three qualities that you have to train; compassion, selflessness, and mindfulness. Mindfulness helps to improve your focus on the task that you are performing, making you productive. It allows you to be present with clients, your people, and other stakeholders. That presence improves loyalty and connectedness and enables the other two qualities. Selflessness is moving away from the ego. If you are selfless as a leader, you are concerned with the needs and interests of your people, of the company, and of the society in general. It increases creativity and engagement. Compassion is about keeping in mind the happiness and well-being of others. A compassionate leader is always looking for ways to improve other people's well-being. Their teams find them trustworthy.

These three qualities make you the kind of leader who enables better health, trust, social cohesion, and performance. In the last twenty years, neuroscientists have found that our brains are neuroplastic/flexible. They are constantly changing across life based on how we use them. This neuroplasticity means that we can treat our brains like we treat our muscles when we go to the gym. It means that if you want to become a more compassionate, selfless, and mindful leader, there are specific exercises that you can do to rewire your brain and allow it to switch from the default way of working to a more productive one. In mindfulness training, you learn to be more aware and focused. Training for selflessness teaches you gratitude and humility, and training for compassion teaches you to look out for others. The strategies at the end of this chapter are based on this research.

To bring these core qualities to your daily leadership, you have to consider your motivation. Why will these qualities be important to you and to your values? Once you answer this question, you can set the intention to grow them. You will begin noticing them as you practice the tips provided later on in the chapter. As you grow in mindfulness, you will become more present. You will be able to refrain from multitasking, especially when engaging with people. Mindful leaders are able to cut through the clutter when they are faced with a challenge and tap into their creative mind.

In the same way, as you grow in selflessness, you will notice that you find it easy to praise your team when they succeed and take responsibility for any setbacks. Selfless leaders speak in terms of 'us' and 'we' rather than 'I' and 'Me.' They notice the contributions of others and they take the time to express gratitude. Finally, a compassionate leader seeks to be useful to others. They are constantly looking to help others and they do not hold back feedback if it will help someone reach their potential. They are also willing to make hard, but wise, calls and execute them with kindness and care.

It is worth noting that gender plays a role in the way these characteristics play out in the workplace or even at home. Many professional women tend to be too other-focused because society and culture have trained them to downplay their accomplishments - assertiveness in women tends to be punished or seen as less competent. Even so, research has found that women can work to overcome their tendencies to be other-focused, as these tendencies can be more harmful than useful. Working on a healthy sense of self and your confidence, combined with the orientation to serve others, helps a great deal. Remember that selflessness does not mean becoming a doormat. It is more about controlling our natural egoistic tendencies so that they do not become a challenge to our effectiveness in leadership.

HOW TO DEVELOP A QUIET MIND

On average, we have about 50,000 thoughts every day, according to research. While thinking is important to great leadership, you need the ability to control and quiet your thoughts if you will lead well. Here are tips that have helped top leaders achieve the same.

- Take time out

For many people, focus is the only thing that cures a chattering mind. When you are focused, it is nearly impossible to entertain thoughts outside of the task at hand. Focused action is your friend, but so are time outs. Every day, spend some time on prayer, meditation, or deep breathing exercises. You can adopt short techniques to use whenever your mind is too loud. Your mind is your most important aspect, so spare time to keep it strong and healthy through stillness.

- Control your fears

There is an acronym that defines fear as 'false evidence appearing real.' It could not be truer than that. If you want your mind to stop hopping between fears, you need to address them. Ask yourself what the worst possible case is and work through it instead of letting fear take hold. In fact, something as simple as naming your fear can give you clarity. When fear shows up, keep yourself grounded in what you are doing instead of re-playing projected possibilities that could or could not come true.

- Take the wheel

There is plenty in life that you cannot control, but that is not your problem. Leave it to the divine. Instead, focus on the thoughts which you can control and on the things in your environment that you can exert influence over. Practicing gratitude can help you with this. Begin each day with gratitude so that it sets the tone for your day. With time, your mind reflexively becomes more positive.

- Release mental attachments

Daniel Gilbert and Matthew Killingsworth, both Harvard psychologists, conducted a study on the unhappy and wandering mind. They found that the mind wanders in response to its biological directive. It wanders because that is how it imagines you will survive longer. You can learn to remove that internal motivation to problem-solve without your conscious permission. That way, you quieten the survival mind and create a feeling of peace. One reliable way to do this is to let go of your mental attachments. Your mental attachments use your mental capital for illogical purposes. They take up processing power and space that you could use for real problems in your life.

By definition, a mental attachment is the exaggerated fear that you will lose a particular benefit, which is often imaginary. Naturally, your mind imagines negative futures and comes up with ways to avoid them. It looks down the road and creates a strategy to create a different outcome. Mental attachments create unnecessary anxiety and stress, and unwanted loops. Letting go of these attachments allows you to use more of your mental capital.

6

TAKE IT ONE STEP AT A TIME

"Concentrate every minute like a Roman – like a man – on doing what's in front of you with precise and genuine seriousness, tenderly, willingly, with justice. And on freeing yourself from all other distractions. Yes, you can – if you do everything as if it were the last thing you were doing in your life, and stop being aimless... You will see how few things you have to do to live a satisfying and reverent life. If you can manage this, that's all even the gods can ask of you." – **Marcus Aurelius.**

It is a common saying, 'take it one step at a time.' Focus on the next thing, they say. Take each day as it comes, but is it that easy? How many times have you, knowing this common saying, still attempted to do so many things, solve so many problems at once? Whenever you begin a new thing, you cannot do everything at the same time and then expect that you will be a master – you do each step as it comes. If you want to start living a fit lifestyle, you don't go to the gym on Monday and do your week's workout in one day. That would be ridiculous! Each morning, you have to ask yourself what you want to achieve and then go to the gym and get it done.

Why then, is the principle so simple and yet so difficult to put into practice in other areas of life? In the gym, you know that if you keep going and if you keep pushing through little steps, one day you will look back and find your starting point miles away, and you will realize just how far you have come. Many years back when I was suffering from depression, I knew I had to change something. In retrospect, I didn't realize how badly I was doing then but I still knew that I needed to make some major changes so that I could get out of the grip of illness. I started doing little things. Every day, I would concentrate on doing just one thing that made me feel better. Eventually, I felt motivated to do it the next day and I started seeing changes brought by my small steps. Of course, that birthed hope and hope is the best catalyst for turning life around.

When you have hope, where you are going becomes much clearer. No challenge will stop you. The next thing you know, your goal is only inches away. Now imagine if I had tried to do everything at once. Imagine if I had pushed myself too hard to work out, for example. I would have gotten overwhelmed. I would have stretched my focus in too many directions and that would have left me overwhelmed and kept me even further from my goal. The destination would have seemed both unclear and unreachable.

A friend of mine once told me that every day, she thinks to herself 'what would the average person do in my situation?' She figured that she was pretty average after factoring in her upbringing, her home, and her circumstances. The average person would likely skip working out for several days. They might skip walking their dog or they might settle for a life of bare minimums. When she figured this out, she would ask herself 'Is that what I want to be? Do I want an average and mundane life? A life of just getting by?' To these questions, her answer was always a resounding no. So, each day, she would figure out one more thing, one more step that the average person would not take and then she would take it.

She is one of the most extraordinary people I know. She goes to the gym and is at the peak of her fitness even though she is over 48 years old. She eats healthy and she is very successful in her career. Just by taking one small step each day more than the average person, she has built a life that we can only admire. Doing just one more thing every day means that she was making small victories and it ensured that she would be feeling good about herself every day. You make this a habit and soon enough, you cannot believe how much trouble you have endured.

The argument of this chapter is that you can learn to endure adversity if you narrow your focus to just one goal. If, instead of focusing on getting fit, getting a promotion, growing your family, and all your other life goals at once, you pick just one goal and focus on it alone for a while. You let it consume you until you have achieved it. Then, you will be able to deal with whatever challenges come your way. Of course, this will demand that you learn to measure success differently. Your success will no longer be that you have achieved that goal. It will be that you have done the small steps that propel you each day toward that goal. If you took just one step today, then at the end of the day, you can be proud because you are closer to your goal.

Taking it one step at a time will demand that you learn to be proud of your little achievements and even prouder when you are eventually able to look back and see how the small actions have compounded. To keep going, you will need to learn to praise yourself along the way, otherwise you lose motivation before you hit the goal. Sounds simple, right? So why is it that many people don't do it? Think about it; how many times have you told yourself that you will do something and then abandoned the plan the minute you encountered a challenge?

Perhaps one of these scenarios will resonate with you. You pick a diet plan and decide that you will stick with it and then halfway through the day, you end up breaking it. Soon enough, you abandon it altogether. Or perhaps, you say you will work hard on a given project but you get distracted by something else and your plan goes out the window. Maybe you say you will start meditating each morning and one of those mornings you leave in a rush so you skip meditation. You skip it again the next day and then the next. Or you say you will keep up with your mail, read more, or declutter your space, but somehow your plans do not get off the ground. What is usually going on in these instances? Is it that you lack discipline? Are we all just hopeless cases, doomed to spend our lives in less-than-ideal situations?

WHY WE DON'T STICK TO ONE THING

In my many years of practicing as a counselor, I found that there is usually more than one reason we don't stick to our plans. The most common reasons for abandoning our goals though, are common to everyone. For starters, it could be that you do not take your goal seriously enough. It is not enough to tell yourself that you will stick to a plan. Most of the time when this is all there is, you are subconsciously assuming that achieving it will be easy and ignoring all past evidence to the contrary. Half commitments do not cut it. Enduring challenges and achieving a goal requires serious effort. Getting into it with partial commitment only guarantees that you will bail out at the first sign of trouble.

Other times we bail out because we forget. We tell ourselves that we will work out every day and we say it with resolve and then the next morning you get so busy you forget. You remember later in the day but you are still busy. The next day you also forget and by the time you remember, you are so disappointed in yourself that you give up. Or perhaps, it is that uncertainty makes you uncomfortable. What if you work out but you don't see the results? When we are faced with a difficult habit, there is a lot of uncertainty surrounding it so you may start finding reasons to procrastinate.

Sometimes, we abandon our goals because something tempts us. There is temptation all around us. Maybe a chocolate cake may not be appealing enough to get you out of your diet plan, but a meetup with a friend instead of putting in more work hours is. There is always something more appealing than what we have to do when we are faced with adversity. The truth, though, is that temptation is just an alternative to discomfort. It is our habitual responses to that discomfort that cause us to give in to temptation. We tend to rationalize our choices and so temptation always rules our response.

You do not have to rationalize temptation though. When something is difficult, rationalizing can also be our way out of it. We start to think, 'what if I don't do what I said I would do?' Our brains are very good at it. Soon enough we convince ourselves that not keeping our word just once won't hurt. 'You worked hard, you deserve a break,' we tell ourselves. 'Tomorrow is just as good a day to get started,' or 'Today is a special occasion, I can make an exception.' At the time, all rationalizations sound reasonable, but they end up sabotaging your plans and your goals. Once you start to believe them, sticking to any plan becomes nearly impossible.

Other times still, we abandon our goals because we renegotiate them. We say that we will do something and then when the time comes to do it, feeling the discomfort of uncertainty, we find another time that is just as good to do it. 'I am tired at the moment, maybe I should take the day off and do it tomorrow,' we may say. Basically, this is a way to try to get out of a difficulty by not attending to it. One of the most harmful things to self-discipline is renegotiating with ourselves. Eventually, you lose trust in your ability to achieve whatever you set out to do.

There are also times that we walk out on our goals because we dislike doing things that we are not very good at, or that don't feel good. For example, you may get out of eating healthy because you don't like the taste of vegetables. Or you could bail out of sending an uncomfortable email to your colleague because you do not like conflict. The magnitude of the problem does not matter – we avoid things we dislike. The problem is that every habit and every difficulty will require that you experience some level of discomfort. We will never stick with anything if we get into the habit of leaving as soon as we feel uncomfortable. We do not need to like everything about something we are experiencing to throw ourselves into it. Resilience demands that we be stronger than that.

Of all the reasons we bail out of our goals, the most significant is that we forget why the goal matters. You take a project very seriously at the start, but then a month later, you have forgotten why it matters and all you can think about it is the discomfort it involves. Soon enough you find yourself thinking that it does not matter if you are committed to it. When we forget the why behind our actions, any challenge is bound to make us bow out. Even when you eventually remember why it matters, you are too disappointed to get back to it. When we falter or fall short of our expectations, it is not a big deal. But when you are used to beating yourself up for it, it sabotages your efforts.

There can never be too many obstacles when you take it one step at a time. Let's say you have started eating healthier. You have a plan for the kind of food you want to eat, but in the morning, you feel hungry and are often in a hurry. You are supposed to scramble tofu but that requires that you chop vegetables, cook, and clean. You figure that there are too many things to do when you are hungry so you grab a coffee and bagel on your way out. This is the big problem when you are attacking everything at once. The challenges feel too high because you have not slowed down and broken them into small manageable steps.

Now imagine creating a healthy shopping list for the kind of food you want to eat. On the day you go shopping, you buy yogurt, fruits, and eggs. In the morning, you wake up only five minutes earlier than your usual time. You scramble eggs and snack on fruit on your way to the office. The same challenges - hunger, time, diet - no longer feel difficult because you took the time to decompose them into small manageable steps - making a shopping list, shopping in advance, waking up 5 minutes earlier, etc. You can break down any problem into its composite parts to make it easier to solve.

So the question is, why do we keep letting obstacles trip us up? Are there no solutions? Of course there are, but you have to consciously decide to implement them and be on the lookout for these obstacles.

BUILDING RESILIENCE STEP BY STEP

The problem is that even when we are committed to working hard on our goals, we have a natural tendency to go back to old habits that feel safe and familiar. This is what makes a permanent lifestyle change difficult. There is research to suggest that the way to go about mastering the different areas of life is counterintuitive. Too many good intentions, practical as they seem, work against you. If you want to master many different habits and integrate them into who you are for good, you have to figure out how you will stay consistent.

Research has proven that you are three times more likely to keep to a habit if you make your plan specific. You have to state where, when, and how you will execute the action. For instance, in one study, researchers asked one group of people to complete the following sentence: 'In the coming week, I will take a minimum of 20 minutes to exercise on (Day) at (time) in (place).' A control group was asked to simply make a similar resolution without any specifics. The researchers found that the people who filled out the statement were more likely to exercise. Psychologists refer to these plans as 'implementation intentions.' You have to state the specifics of when you will implement a specific action.

The findings of that research have been proven and repeated several times with different groups of varying demographics and across goals. For example, people who set implementation intentions for recycling were found to actually begin recycling. The same was found to be true for stopping negative habits like smoking. However, research following up on the subject has found that setting intentions only works provided you focus on one thing at a time. People who tried to achieve different goals at the same time were found to be less committed and less likely to succeed than people who shifted their focus to just one goal. This is an important caveat to bear in mind so let me reiterate – developing a specific plan for where, how, and when you will do something will make you more likely to follow through when you encounter challenges, but it works only if you focus on one thing at a time.

What happens when your focus is on one thing at a time? A different set of research findings helps us to answer this question. When you begin solving a new problem or learning a new habit, you need plenty of conscious effort to do it. Given time, the habit becomes easier. Eventually, it becomes the new normal as the process grows more mindless and automated. Researchers call this process 'automaticity.' It is the ability to do something or perform an action without thinking about all the necessary steps taken to accomplish it. It allows the action to become habitual.

The thing with automaticity is that it only happens because of lots of practice and repetition. The more reps you invest, the more automatic an action becomes. While researching automaticity, scientists asked people to create a habit of taking a ten-minute walk after breakfast. They found that at the start, automaticity was very low. After a month of consistency, the habit became routine. 60 days later, the process was already automated. It is important to note that there is a tipping point beyond which habits become more automatic. That tipping point varies, though, based on factors such as your genetics, the level of difficulty of the habit, and your environment.

Even so, according to one study, it takes an average of 66 days of consistent repetition to make a habit automatic. Do not put too much emphasis on the number, though. An average suggests a range. Besides, the study considered a wide range of participants across a wide range of factors. The only reasonable conclusion is that it will take you a couple of months for a habit to stick.

So, what is the point of taking one step at a time and how does it contribute to resilience? Taking it one step at a time allows you to change your life without overhauling your entire life. It makes it more likely that when you meet a challenge, because your focus is narrow and your view is clear, you stay the course. Let's review the facts we know from science. You are three times more likely to stick to a habit if you are particular about where you will do it, how, and when. This is the implementation intention. Secondly, your focus should be on one thing and one thing alone. Implementation intentions only work if you are improving one habit at a time. Finally, a habit becomes more automatic the more you practice it. On average, it will take a minimum of two months to automate a habit.

These three facts bring us to the punchline of this chapter; the counterintuitive way to keep at a goal and endure despite the challenge. According to research, the best way to change your circumstances is by not changing all of your circumstances. Rather, focus only on one specific part. Work on it until you have sufficiently mastered it and fully integrated it into your life. Then, go ahead and repeat the same process with another part of the problem. Simply put, the only way to master more things in the end, is to focus on one thing at the moment.

7

CONNECT WITH YOUR TRUE SELF

'No person is free who has not mastered himself.'
– Epictetus.

T here are times when the thing barring our endurance is our lack of connection to who we are. In those periods, captured by our pseudo-selves, we end up pursuing goals that do not truly align with ourselves. Expectedly, when we encounter a challenge, we fold. That is why authenticity is a key part of resilience. Being authentic feels wonderful; it is energizing, exhilarating, and freeing. However, the process of discovering your genuine self can be extremely difficult. For millennia, philosophers, scientists, artists, and spiritualists have argued over the question 'Who am I?' It is a lifelong process to find the answer, but it need not be challenging.

There are a few things you need to figure out before you can be an authentic leader. Your true needs, beliefs, desires, feelings, characteristics, and thoughts are expressed when you are your most authentic self. Who would you be if you were not concerned about the negative effects of your actions? That is your authentic self. So, the first thing to consider is how real you actually are in your interactions. The advice to 'be yourself' strikes many people as impossible and unrealistic. Understanding the meaning of authenticity in detail is one way to demystify it. From there, you can determine the behavioral areas where you can demonstrably and visibly display your authenticity, and then assess whether you are doing so.

Once you are familiar with the various facets of authenticity, consider how you present yourself in each one. Are the interactions you have with people real or fake? Decide what characteristics make up your genuine self, then try to live more often in those. Do you come across as authentic while talking with people, or do you try to hide your characteristics to fit in? We conceal different aspects of ourselves in an effort to fit in, whether we are aware of it or not.

Sometimes we fail to convey our emotions. Because we are concerned that the emotions are inappropriate, we hide our wrath, contempt, or terror. In other situations, we try to hide our joy or surprise. We do this through our verbal and nonverbal communication. However, there is freedom to be found when you have a clear idea of your desired behavior in various contexts and what would define your real self. Knowing that clues you in on how you can act authentically. This chapter talks about authenticity and defines it. You will get an in-depth knowledge of what an authentic leader can do, how to achieve this sense of authenticity, and how it contributes to your ability to persevere.

WHAT IS AUTHENTICITY?

An authentic leader is concerned with projecting who they really are and embodying the things they believe. On social media, there are many influencers who appear nice to their followers, but who are different when they are not trying to impress their followers. Some are inconsiderate and cruel to their employees. No leader who deserves their influence should live a double life. A true leader does not have inauthentic sides.

If you have different (and seemingly opposing) sides to your personality, it is a sign that you still have some personal work to do. The effective leader does not have a work personality and another one when they get home. They do not have to try to come across a certain way to their colleagues and a different way to their managers. Even when dealing with the pressure that comes with a challenge or when they are pressured to act out of alignment, they do not yield. Authenticity is not about playing a role. It is being. Basically speaking, authenticity is about being sincere, not a copycat. The word implies that you embody your true self in whatever role you play. It means that you draw on your morals, principles, and values to create a guiding compass for how you deal with challenges. You use a personal compass, not an external one.

Many people wrongly assume that you become a good leader by copying the styles and traits other great leaders have, but that is not the case. True, you can learn from other great leaders, but authenticity in leadership is about acting in ways that draw from who you really are in all situations. This means that you have to be highly self-aware. Your focus is both the result and the process. Your team sees your true personality and that inspires them to be who they are and to work to improve their skills. Authenticity in leadership is not about copying trends. It is not about following fads even though some fads appear successful. It is about understanding what matters and then giving yourself to those no matter what comes against you.

When you are authentic in your leadership, you follow your heart. You lead from within. You only go after the things that you have an unquenchable passion for, which means that you stay with them for the long-term, which is where authenticity meets resilience. Authentic leaders have a passionate mission that they dedicate their whole lives to. Of course, the goal is not something like 'making money' or 'creating another team.' It is about forming relationships that will last, with people who will help them achieve their dreams and goals. Authenticity is marked by genuineness, but there are other qualities that people who are authentic in their leadership share. For instance, their lives are lived out in ways that make them trustworthy. They accept responsibility for who they are and they own up to their mistakes. They are:

- Self-aware and true – They know their strengths, limitations, and are familiar with their emotions. Their teams get to see their real selves. They do not hide their frailties out of a desire to manage other people's perception of them. Rather, they accept their humanity.
- Mission-driven – For authentic leaders, work is not about power, money, or ego. They work with a genuine desire to help people and to achieve their goals.
- Lead from within – True, authentic leaders use reason in their leadership, but they also let others see their emotions and their vulnerability. They communicate with empathy and directly, something which connects them with their employees.
- Always see the big picture – In their daily activities, authentic leaders do not lose sight of the big picture. They know how the details contribute to the overarching

goal. They make their choices with that goal in mind, which produces results both in the moment and in the future.

For you to embody these traits, you have to commit to continuous self-improvement and learning so that you can understand yourself and the people around you. You have to let go of your ego. You know that if you work from your heart, you have the ability to sustainably empower others. Remember that there is no one model leader. Even the best leaders have unique skills, traits, and style combinations that constitute authenticity. The goal of this part is not to give you a template to copy, but to help you find these things within yourself and grow them in alignment with your values. In a lot of ways, authenticity is about having your heart, head, and speech aligned. It is observing a consistency between what you feel, say, think, and do. That inspires people. It builds trust.

BUILDING AUTHENTICITY

Building authenticity is a process of discovery and nurture. It calls for you to be courageous and honest with yourself. You have to reflect on your life choices and experiences, understand what drives you, and then own your story. The good thing about being someone who leads with authenticity is that it will be worth the effort. It will balance out your life in ways you could not have predicted. It will leave a lasting impact on anyone you interact with. But how do you discover your real self? How do you stay true to that when you are pressured to be different? How do you become self-aware enough to trust the innate wisdom in your value system?

For starters, you have to do a self-appraisal to know your strengths and weaknesses. When you know what you are good at, you know where to invest your energies. You know in what direction to pivot when faced with a challenge so that you tackle it from a different angle instead of throwing in the towel. You will know when to communicate your concerns and you will no longer be blinded by your weaknesses because you will be working to improve them. Understanding your limits will help you create a team that trusts your capabilities. Such a team needs a culture of giving and receiving feedback, though. You have to be comfortable with the fact that you are part of a network and at one point or another, someone will know better than you do. To be an effective leader is to keep an open mind. It is to accept constructive criticism and integrate it.

Secondly, you build authenticity by practicing emotional intelligence. Emotional intelligence is in part about managing how you react and understanding other people's reactions, and using that knowledge to create relationships that last. Everyone will have different responses to adversity. Some people in your team will follow their impulse and have outbursts of anger. Emotional intelligence will help you not to be those people. It equips you to respond with pride and integrity. You know that it is not the end of the world if something bad happens. There is always a way out. When you are on top of your emotions, you can share your concerns calmly and intelligibly.

Finally, building authenticity is about being mindful. Take some time and listen to your own thoughts. Tune in to your body and observe its sensations and what they are trying to communicate. Mindfulness helps you to know what you are feeling and how you should respond to your impulses. It puts you back in touch with your values, thoughts, and beliefs especially after distress, helping you to be authentic. It keeps your mind open to the backgrounds and opinions of others. It helps you to focus on what you are doing.

TOOLS FOR BUILDING AUTHENTICITY

By now it is clear that discovering who you really are and weaving it into your leadership style takes work. It takes self-reflection to learn your values and demands that you look deep, even beyond social conditioning. Mostly, it takes courage to stay true to the person you discover. There are three tools that you can use in this section. The first one will help you in the process of self-discovery and the second one will help you figure out whether you are acting authentically. It is easy to lose track, so when you are faced with a challenge and you find yourself internally resisting it and wanting to quit, it is a good practice to first confirm that it aligns with who you are before anything else. Use the third exercise for that. All the three activities hinge upon self-reflection. Be sure to be honest with yourself.

1. Use the authenticity principle

The authenticity principle lists seven behavioral dimensions to your decision making. They include: the way you express your feelings; the extent to which you will refrain from saying what you feel; how you use nonverbal communication such as gestures, touch, posture, and facial expressions; your choice of words, whether they are formal or informal, your vocabulary, etc.; how you speak - your pitch, pace, volume, and accent; and how you present yourself before other people – which clothes do you choose to wear, what's your style? It also includes the things you reveal about your values, ideas, and opinions, and your treatment of other people.

The point of this exercise is for you to use the seven dimensions to guide you to self-discovery. Find a place that's quiet and conducive for thinking and set aside some time. Carry a notebook and pen, or your laptop. Get rid of all the distractions, reflect on, and answer the following questions, providing as many details as you can. Answer the questions for each dimension.

- If your behavior had no consequences, how would this dimension look like for you?
- When do you remember feeling inauthentic in this dimension? What was the context? How did you act and why?

After answering these questions, think about your answers analytically. Of the seven dimensions, which one matters the most to you? What things can you not compromise on, and what are you flexible about?

2. Use questions to self-reflect

The first exercise equips you to understand yourself better. It creates a background for making empowered choices. This second exercise provides more clarity and meaning. It will lead you to understand how authenticity and speaking the truth are connected without crossing your personal boundaries. To perform it, simply answer 'yes' or 'no' without overthinking. When you finish, think about your answers and figure out what you learn about your values from them.

- *Can you share your fears and struggles openly?*
- *Do you apologize many times when you make a mistake?*
- *Do you pass blame when you make mistakes?*
- *If someone asks for your opinion, do you share everything?*
- *Are you constantly trying to prove how right your perspective is?*

3. Test your authenticity on the regular

You have not mastered authenticity until you are able to stay true to yourself every day. When you are out of alignment, you have to pause, rediscover, and reconnect with your true self. This process increases your self-confidence, your belief system, and your ability to persevere in adversity. You regain your creativity and motivation. Use the following questions whenever you need to figure out whether you are behaving in alignment. Bear in mind that as you answer these questions, with time your true self will perk up. Continue with your exploration and check in regularly. You will start seeing the difference between your true self and yourself in survival mode.

- How easy did you find it to make a decision?

When you are in alignment, you always sense what is the best path forward for you. The different factors that make decision making difficult do not stop existing, but somehow you know what you should do. Whenever you are struggling to make a decision, it is because there are things hiding the simplicity of your authentic choice. Note that you are inauthentic when you make choices based on the desire to avoid confrontation or the fear of other people's judgment.

- Do you speak the truth at all times?

How often do you bend the truth? How honest are you, for example, when telling a friend what happened to you? Do your stories seem to change every time you replay them in your mind? Do your feelings cause you to re-interpret events? Your authentic self does not need to lie. When you lie, you are choosing the fear of consequences or your insecurity. If you regularly feel the need to lie, you are not taking responsibility for your actions, choices, or mistakes, and you are likely unhappy with them. Your true self does not hide from, or hide, the truth. It allows yourself to step out at all times.

- Are your actions true to your values?

What things occupy your days? At any moment in your day, pause and ask yourself whether what you are doing is true to what you believe. If your answer is 'yes,' you are walking in authenticity. If not, you need to course correct and recommit to your values.

- Are you criticizing yourself more?

We tend to criticize ourselves more when we know that what we are doing is not right. If your inner voice is getting overly critical, it may be a sign that you have left the path of authenticity. Your true voice is soft. It is clear, supportive, and kind. Ignore the criticism in your mind for a while and listen to the quiet voice underneath and then follow it back to the right path.

- How do you answer when asked who you are?

If you notice that your answer to who you are is what you do, there is a problem. The authentic you is not just your accomplishments or your work. It is about the person you are without those external trappings. It is the core of who you are. If you cannot explain that to someone, it is a sign that you have lost touch. Take the time and remind yourself of who you are and the things you love.

- If you could choose again, would you choose what you are doing at the moment?

Whenever you are unsatisfied with the things you are doing every day, there is trouble. The things you do need to match with what you want to do, otherwise you are guided by inauthenticity. When walking in your true self, you pick what suits you best. Even when you are doing things you do not necessarily enjoy, you know their utility and value their contribution to your goals. You know you are being true when your choices make you fall deeply in love with your life.

- Are you feeling fearful, stressed, confused, or anxious?

We all have low points. It is normal to experience stress after an argument, for example, but if you are constantly feeling anxious, fearful, confused, or stressed and you cannot explain it, you have fallen out of tune. You need to do some soul searching and return to your true self.

- How often do you feel curious?

Curiosity cannot be divorced from authenticity. When you are curious, you are open to the world, you explore it and experience it deeply. You are attentive to details and you relish even the small things. It may be a sign that you are no longer being authentic if you have stopped asking questions. You may have grown content and on the path to completely veering off. Your authenticity demands that you are constantly engaged and involved.

8

LEAN ON YOUR SUPPORT
SYSTEM

'Try to enjoy the great festival of life with other men!' -
Epictetus.

I n 2016, the unimaginable happened to Christine. She wanted to help someone she cared about; someone who was sick and hiding it. She went to his house determined to carry out a rescue operation that she imagined would end at the emergency room. Instead, she ended up on a trip to the morgue. She found that her ex-husband had died on his living room floor. The reason? Drug addiction. It was undoubtedly the most traumatic event in her life, and the lives of her two then teenage children. She was with them in the car and she had unwittingly given them a front-row seat to their father's death.

It took her two years to settle her ex-husband's estate that was in probate. That meant that in those two years, her trauma could not be fully resolved as she continued to live in what she described as an 'unending emergency.' If you had asked her then, she would have told you that they would never really recover. She thought that their lives would always be stained by that tragedy. Yet, when I met her in 2020, she was among the happiest people I had ever met. It was in the midst of a pandemic when we first spoke and she thought that those awful times in her life had been training for the social and political upheaval that followed the pandemic.

Christine says that from that experience, she learned that you can never know what is going to happen next. At best, you can plan, but the future is out of your hands. What you can know for sure is that you will cope better with life's unexpected arrows and slings if you face your difficulties alongside the people you love. She says that nothing helped her navigate the difficulties of grief more than social support. How we navigate a traumatic event or a crisis depends, in many ways, on our resilience. Your resilience is dictated by an interplay between factors like your personal history, genetics, the situational context, and your environment. So far, research has found that genetics contribute the least to resilience while social support contributes the most.

According to a report by the National Opinion Research Center, 92% of Americans have gone through at least one major negative life event. Maybe you got divorced, lost a job, or had to deal with an injury. To put it mildly, life can be hard. Even though everyone suffers these negative events, we all respond differently. There are people who seem to find it easy to shake off what life deals them while others develop stress, PTSD, general anxiety, and substance abuse.

Another study by the National Institute of Health found that there are two major factors associated with resilience when faced with adversity, and both are in your control. The researchers looked into one of the worst traumas people can undergo – physical assault. They interviewed 159 women who had experienced physical abuse. They wanted to gauge the respondents' past and current levels of PTSD and other mental conditions associated with such trauma, as well as how much social support and resilience they had and their quality of life.

Researchers found that 79% of the respondents did not suffer PTSD after the assault. Most of them suffered depression in response, though – 30%. The researchers then went further and divided the women into categories – those who had no psychiatric disorder diagnosis, those who had been diagnosed in the past but had recovered, and those who were currently diagnosed. When they analyzed the data they collected, they found one major difference between the group who never had a diagnosis or those who recovered, and the group that was currently diagnosed – social support and mastery.

In this context, mastery refers to the level of control people perceive they have over the circumstances in their lives. This differs from optimism or the expectation of a positive outcome. Mastery is the better predictor of resilience than optimism. Other studies have found that mastery reduces PTSD symptoms in veterans and in women who have suffered violence from their intimate partners. The more mastery you have, the better your quality of life, and the less your chances of disease mortality. A similar study of 4,000 adults found that higher mastery was a predictor of better health, more satisfaction in life, and less depressive symptoms, regardless of how well they were doing socioeconomically. The lead researcher in the study stated that a sense of personal control over your life is central to psychological adjustment more so after assault, which can consume you with feelings of powerlessness and uncertainty.

The second factor that the researchers identified was just as crucial. Respondents who had a strong social support were found to be less likely to develop psychological disorders, and when they did, they recovered. Conversely, respondents who experienced critical, unreceptive, and unsupportive responses from family, friends, or coworkers were at a high risk of developing psychiatric disorders. The researchers concluded that the negative impact was caused by the attempts to discourage open communication, which raises suppression and cognitive avoidance of memories related to the trauma. It results in self-blame and withdrawal. In this chapter, you will learn how social support makes you more resilient, and find ways to build and improve your support system.

HOW SOCIAL SUPPORT MAKES YOU RESILIENT

Until recently, researchers did not always emphasize social support as an important contributor to resilience. Instead, they placed an emphasis on studying personal qualities. For example, research in the 1980s and 1990s found that people were happier when they had a strong purpose in life and when they believed that they could control their lives. These are the same factors that helped them recover after a disaster. These personality factors have been found to create some sort of immunity against disasters like economic hardship or the loss of a loved one.

As time went by, research around resilience became varied and complex. Some of the research suggests that resilience looks different based on the kind of hardship in question, so that some protective factors do not help in all the circumstances. The factors were also subject to individual constitution. It is also true that resilience does not stay the same across time. It is a fluctuating trait affected by environmental and developmental changes. It was in the increasing complexity of this research that scientists found out that support plays a significant role in resilience.

One resilience researcher says that social support in all its forms matters when you are facing a challenge, whether it is emotional or instrumental. We may think that changing ourselves is all we need to face adversity and come out stronger, but positive relationships and a supportive environment are just as significant. That is why keeping good social relationships when life is alright is a winning strategy. Other research into the population at large has proven that positive relationships at any period in life predict that the individual is less likely to be depressed later. Researchers even recommend social relationships as a protective measure for older adults.

Social support is so important because it reduces stress reactions. Even the memory of a good relationship is enough to reduce your stress levels. A different study looked at the responses of wives who felt very connected with their spouses, and found that they were less reactive to stress. The research overwhelmingly concludes that when you are going through a difficult time, you need to lean into your support system. It does take a village to move beyond a disaster.

HOW TO BUILD AND STRENGTHEN YOUR SUPPORT SYSTEM

When you hear someone speak of a healthy support system, you may imagine something like the characters in a comedy show like *Friends* – you and your friends hanging out in a coffee shop, talking about your day. Yes, that could be a support system. Friendships are an important element of the support system, but its roots have to go deeper than that. They have to include both your professional and personal life so that you get a wide range of outlets if one part is not working. It is called a system for a reason. For example, what do you do when you need emotional support because you got into an argument with your friend if you do not have other friends? A healthy support system gives you many resources and outlets for easing your stress.

The essence of a support system is for you to have a safe space to process your struggles, thoughts, and emotions. This is a critical part of resilience building. When you process your struggles effectively, you are clear headed enough to find a way forward that does not involve quitting. It is important to note that a healthy and solid support system is made up of people who are important to you, but who also feel the same way about you. The relationships need to be reciprocal. However, there is no system for tallying the give and take in a supportive relationship. All support is given and accepted freely. That is the only way you can enjoy the benefits that positive social relationships have to offer. The following are ways you can build your support system and strengthen it.

- Figure out your expectations

Take some time to think about what you want from your support network. Do you need friends who help you to unwind after a stressful day and who will listen to your worries? Or are you trying to upgrade your professional life and you need support? If your situation is the latter, you may want to find support from coworkers or from people working in your industry. There is a caveat, though. While it is critical to focus on the kind of support you are looking for, you need a wide range of support in different flavors. Your current mental health and needs may change in six months or so. Conceptualize yourself like a tent – if you only have one leg staked in, the wind might blow you away. Secure all your poles and when the storm comes, you will be able to weather it.

That said, you may prioritize a type of support depending on your current needs, whether it is deep friendships, an assorted network of acquaintances within the same industry, or professional friendships. Do not let the others lag behind though, because you never know what trouble is waiting around the corner. Always remember that the support system you build is always a work in progress. There are people in your support system who may not be available when you need them or who may have outgrown the role. That is okay. People change with time. They move on. So should your support system. Be open enough to make changes when you need to.

- Strengthen your bonds with friends and family

Sometimes, people who can offer you the kind of support you need in adversity are people right under your nose – the friends you know well and your family make for excellent cheerleaders. If you are feeling gloomy, you can call them and they will pick up. Understandably, we have not always done a good job of keeping in touch through the years. Maybe you made friends in college but you drifted apart after leaving, so you only see each other occasionally. Perhaps your family lives a state away and you have been lax about visiting and calling.

You cannot build a healthy support system with them unless you start reaching out. The good thing is that these relationships already exist. You just need to invest in them a little more to strengthen them. If your family or friends live in a different city, video chats and phone calls are a good idea. Plan for visits as well if you can afford it. If your friends are in the same city, consider planning dates around things you have in common. Revitalizing your relationships will require vulnerability, but that's good practice. All effective support networks need you to open up, and that can be uncomfortable if you are not used to it.

- Build up on your interests

Sometimes, it is not possible to build on the relationships we have with family and friends. Or it could be that you want support from someone who is physically close. That's a tough call, but it is still doable. In such a case, you have two goals – first, you want to make friends so that you have someone you can confide in when you feel lonely or when you are in need. Secondly, you want an outlet that will motivate you to get out of the house and get active instead of sitting in and sulking.

If that is you, ask yourself what activities you enjoy. Do you enjoy watching soccer? Are you into cross-stitching? Whatever your interest, get in touch with like-minded people around you. Join a knitting group, sign up for a hiking community, join a gaming team. Do not get upset or frustrated if you do not make many friends from the get go. It is okay to feel nervous, and it is okay to take time to build upon a friendship. Consistent and regular interaction will help you to ease into the relationship and start feeling comfortable. Even if you do not end up meeting your next best friend, you can still have a good time and enjoy the stress relief that comes from being engaged.

- Expand your professional networks

As a career-minded person, you need a strong professional support system. True, you can still talk to your close friends about work-related stress, but you may have to offer a lot of background information for them to understand and relate. Besides, the level of support someone who is not in your industry may offer is minimal. To expand your professional network, interact with people within your company and outside of it. Your coworkers are a valuable resource that you can access every day, but you will be in a tight spot if your frustration has to do with job hunting. You also need other human resources that support your general career needs. Sign up for, and attend, professional meetups, happy hours, and networking events.

- Create a personal support structure

Support systems by nature rely on others, but it also helps to create a personal support structure that will help you during times when no one in your support system is available. A support structure accounts for things like how you unwind when you have had a bad day, or how you deal with your feelings when you are overwhelmed. The point is to know how to give yourself support. Make sure that self-care is a priority to you. Maybe that means you have a space in your house for meditating, or a prompted journal, or maybe it means that you go out and exercise. Whatever the case, have a way of caring for yourself.

9

APPLY REASON

"Reason gives each side time to plead; moreover, she herself demands adjournment, that she may have sufficient scope for the discovery of the truth; whereas anger is in a hurry: reason wishes to give a just decision; anger wishes its decision to be thought just. The sword of justice is ill-placed in the hands of an angry man." — **Seneca.**

When was the last time you responded to a challenge emotionally? Do you remember letting anger or despair or whatever other negative feeling you experienced get the best of you? Was it the reason you quit trying? Our emotions are strong. If we do not learn to order them, they can have us starting projects and leaving them halfway done because we encountered adversity. They can stunt us rather than push us to grow in the face of adversity.

Emotions are not simple. Whenever you feel something, your body starts to physiologically change. You also experience a chemical release and eventually, a behavioral response. This process involves many systems and steps working together. It calls to play your limbic system, neurotransmitters, and major organs. Your limbic system is the most primordial part of your brain. It is said to have been the first to evolve in mammals. It is made up of old neural pathways which activate your emotions to respond to stimuli. It also uses the autonomic nervous system to control your fight or flight response.

The fight or flight response came from the need to make choices based on our feelings. As the body gets pumped with adrenaline and the heart begins racing, we prepare to react. Your body tries to decide whether you stay to fight the predator or you flee to a safe place. We can still feel this response even today. When you are confronted for not taking out the trash, you might experience the fight or flight response as your adrenaline begins flooding your system. Your heart rate increases and so does your breathing. The hairs on your arms stand and your hands start feeling clammy as you decide whether you will retreat or argue your case.

The sensations in our bodies as we respond to our emotions very often feel similar to one another. Think about feeling your cheeks flush, your palms sweating, and your heart beating in your chest. It could be that you feel this way while seated at your dentist's waiting room, or it could be that you are excited to see your loved ones after a long separation – you still react the same way physiologically. How we interpret these emotions is our logical brain trying to rationalize our responses and describe them as feelings. We account for the context and then we put a label on our emotions.

However, we do not label our emotions in the same way. Our bodies release different chemicals in response to an environmental trigger. Because of this, everyone reacts to situations differently, by nature. Have you ever watched someone getting berated in a meeting but facing their situation with a simple raised brow? Or have you ever seen someone receive bad news with composure?

Yet, some people will raise their voice or shed tears if they are berated in a meeting, for example. Our responses are defined by the way our neurons network. At the same time, our genetic predispositions and our past experiences also affect our brain chemistry and our physiological responses, which then determine the way we react in different circumstances – like someone showing up at your door unannounced or canceling a meeting at the last minute.

Sometimes our emotions even seem like they are an irrational response. Our brains have evolved with one goal – to keep us alive. We may interpret emotions as negative or positive, but the most primordial parts of our brains developed for the sake of survival. Our emotions evolved to communicate function and navigate our interactions with our environment in a safe way.

Originally, our fear responses were a tactic for survival. They served to warn us when there was potential danger – like our innate unease and fear around snakes and spiders. Think about the feeling of disgust – what purpose does it serve? It warns us that food may be dangerous. The same is true for our other emotions. They are responses to social interactions which keep us as part of a group because we are by nature social beings. As we evolved, we had to rely on our tribes to help our survival by collaborating to find shelter and food.

Anger is also a protective emotion. It is a response to a perceived social threat or a dominance signal. Pride helps us to improve our social status and shame is meant to lower our social standing. These emotions keep the social world and the environment in a safe balance. They inform our choices of who to care about, who to trust, and who to follow. Almost always, we are fundamentally motivated by happiness and sadness. Sadness comes from loss and has the biological purpose of motivating recovery after loss, whether it is experienced in a young child lost in the supermarket who then has to look for their mother, or in an adult trying to find a new job because they are unsatisfied with their current one.

The ultimate human emotion, though, is happiness. We are all always looking for it. When you sit with your friends around a campfire and share stories, you feel happy because you have the resources that your primordial brain is looking for – you have social security, food, and comfort. We are naturally drawn to happiness because the emotion is the way your brain's reward system finds environments that are free from threat. Any healthy human brain will cope with sadness when you have no social bonds. It will communicate with the people you love and can regulate your emotions even if you are not feeling especially positive. The next time you have to say goodbye, look out for your emotions. Our bodies have created them to keep us alive. Our feelings and emotions are really what make us human, but it also means that they are not always right in their assessment of reality.

THE SCIENCE OF EMOTION IS STILL DEVELOPING

As it turns out, emotions are your brain's best guess of what a bodily sensation means, and the guess is guided by your past experiences. Your brain comes up with the guess very fast – so fast that your emotions feel like they are an uncontrollable reaction happening to you. Yet, emotions are actually made by you. For the longest time, scientists thought that our emotions were caused by different brain circuits, one for anger, one for fear, another for happiness, and so forth.

They imagined that these circuits get triggered automatically and they create a particular bodily state, facial expression, and physical actions. For instance, if you saw a spider, your fear circuit would be activated and so your eyes would widen, your heartbeat would increase, and you would get ready to run. They imagined that a specific emotion was a chain reaction of different but coordinated events, and it happened reliably enough to show when someone was feeling it.

As researchers investigated this, their findings did not support the assumption. They found that emotion is tied to the entire brain. It uses your past experiences to interpret information from your whole body. For example, if your heart is beating fast, your brain combines that piece of data with what is happening outside, say you are in a fast-moving car, and concludes that the key emotion is fear, because there is potential danger. The same fast heart beat, this time outside your doctor's office, leads the brain to conclude that you are experiencing anxiety. In another situation, say you are watching your lover come into a room, your brain may construct your emotion as excitement because your heart is pounding. When you are exercising, a pounding heart may be fatigue. The meaning your brain creates helps it to decide what the body should do next to keep you safe.

Yet, even with this new understanding of how emotion works, science still has a long way to go. There are scientists who give their lives to studying brain circuits for actions like freezing when in danger, trying to figure out how emotion informs that action. Other studies claim that people all over the world express similar facial movements for the same emotion. There are even companies claiming that they have algorithms for machine learning that detect emotion from scowls and smiles. Yet, these algorithms can only detect muscle movements. They are not able to convey the emotional meaning we attach to context. Data shows, for example, that people living in urban large-scale cultures do not scowl in anger as much as those who live in rural cultures.

Besides, there are many reasons people scowl other than anger. Sometimes people scowl because they are trying to concentrate. Other times they are just constipated. The evidence for the universality of emotional expressions is still wanting. The point here is, even though there is much more known about emotion, there is still a lot of room for research to help us understand our emotional reactions. Even so, we can learn from history how people thought of emotions and how they used reason to keep going no matter the hardship they faced. After all, the goal here is to learn how reason can help us grow more resilient.

REASON AND EMOTION IN DECISION-MAKING

We commonly assume that our emotions interfere with rational thinking. Plato talked about reason and emotion as two horses pulling one cart in opposite directions. The way we look at decision making in modern days is in many ways affected by Platonic thinking. We commonly endorse that disconnect between emotion and reason. For example, when we face a challenge that makes us feel uncomfortable, we are quick to conclude that the discomfort means you should quit. However, it could mean that something you are doing is not working, and that you need to change course and keep going, or pummel on despite the discomfort. In our understanding of how our emotions and reason work, we maintain that one system is automatic and emotional while the other is controlled. The automatic system does things quickly and makes many mistakes. The controlled system keeps a watchful eye over what's happening and makes changes when needed. It acts like a parent, reining in our impulses and overriding our quick judgments.

We can all agree that emotions are powerful experiences, but they are typically short lived. Sometimes they cause us to do things that we regret later. Today we feel very angry because of something a colleague did and we want to berate her. Tomorrow, we come to work wishing our actions had been more rational regardless of how compelling our desire was at the time. Emotions have the ability to transform desires and goals in the heat of the moment and they can lead us to choices that do not serve us in the long-run. As it turns out, when you do something you don't want to do, you are irrational, and so we conclude that emotions make us irrational.

The struggle between emotion and reason is easy to conceptualize. But we have to ask the question – do our emotions always lead us astray? Evidently, they exist to guide us away from pain and toward pleasure. The goal of our emotions is for us to gain the good and avoid the bad in any given environment. In a way, our decisions resemble gambles when we buy a new house, invest in a company, or get married. There is always a chance that our choices will not work out as well as we hope. We need the ability to judge the risks that are worth taking, and it is emotions that help us in making the judgments.

The solution to the emotion versus reason conundrum is much closer to how the stoics saw the two. As far as they were concerned, the two are very important, but reason is the chief. According to Seneca, reason allows you to see both sides of an issue. It gives all the sides time to plead their case and then decides the way forward. It is fully committed to discovering the truth. Emotions like anger will be in a hurry to come up with a decision, but rarely will those decisions be just. To make just decisions, you have to rely on reason. When I talk of justice here, I mean making choices that are good for you now and in the future, and that are good for the people involved. The way to not quit in the heat of emotion is to allow yourself room to explore all the alternatives and then judge based on reason.

APPLY REASON

- Apply reason to stress

Whenever you are confronted with adversity, it is understandable to feel stressed. Even so, stress does not have to drive your way forward. As Marcus Aurelius put it, you have control over your mind. Knowing and living it will give you strength. If you think about it, we know this truth instinctively. Our minds make our emotions. Our emotions are not something happening to us that we have no sway over. We may not be able to control those factors causing the stress, but we can certainly control our response to it. How then, do you reason with your stress? Take some time and write everything that is stressing you. Make sure you separate the things within your control and those that you cannot control. Once you have your full list, take care of what you can control and let the rest go.

- Apply reason to anger

Another natural and seemingly automatic response to adversity is anger. Sometimes we are angry at ourselves, but more often, we are angry with others for their contribution to the trouble we are in. Seneca has something to say to such anger. According to him, if someone is angry, you needn't do anything other than give them time. They soon come to understand what they have done and become their own critic. Anger is a tough emotion because you can order yourself out of it and find that you are not good at obeying your own orders. In such cases, take Seneca's advice. Give yourself time and you will find that you are your best critic.

The next time you get angry at something or someone, instead of lashing out or making a decision quickly, take time off. That is applying reason. Reason will tell you that after you have calmed down, you do not want to feel regret or shame over your actions. It will stop you from acting on your anger. Instead, meditate on the ways you can use your angry energy in productive ways. Remember that you can never avoid feeling angry, but you can avoid letting it bully you.

- Apply reason to relationships

Sometimes, quitting in response to difficulties will be justified, especially if you know they could have been avoided if someone else did their part. We cannot ignore the fact that there will be times when relational difficulties are the reason we want to quit. When those times come, though, stoic wisdom can come to the rescue. Marcus Aurelius advised his students to constantly remind themselves that people are difficult. They will often ignore what is good and choose evil. That should not surprise you. Instead, it should be something you bring to memory so that you approach people knowing that anything is possible, but you still have a choice when it comes to how you deal with them.

Reason will tell you that even though people are difficult, you do not have to be like them. You can choose to do the right thing anyway. You can choose to always do right. It is not within our domain to influence people's actions and thoughts, just our own. Make a deliberate choice to stay committed to influencing yours in the right direction at all times. Commit to showing up as the best version of yourself.

AFTERWORD

Looking at people who live a creative and successful life, exerting positive influence on those around them, we can see elements of understanding, expertise, passion, and most of all, resilience. What is easy to miss is the different things that have to be at play within to make them as they are. What principles govern their mind and behavior? When they encounter failure or adversity, how are they able to adapt and respond appropriately? What is their philosophy?

This book has attempted to help you look closer into their minds and see how things inside translate to what you can see outside. It has drawn from the deep wisdom of the stoics with the sole hope that it will help you become better, live better, and lead better despite the inevitable trials of life. All the nine principles in this book borrow from stoic wisdom. The stoics were concerned with living a happy life and becoming better as a person, and you can see those concerns trickle in every one of the laws.

In chapter 1, you learnt to be strict with yourself and to be tolerant with others. You learnt how delicate a balance it is to be strict. How do you practice strictness with yourself without tyrannizing yourself? After all, tyranny may work for a moment, but it backfires in the long run. The solution – to negotiate with yourself and treat yourself like you are someone you care about, and that you genuinely want to see do well. How does that help you become resilient? It helps you to befriend yourself, which is what you need to move through adversity.

In the second chapter, you were encouraged to face reality. Our brains have a way of interpreting facts to give us the reality we wish for, rather than what is. We have biases that blind us to some realities, and we cannot live and lead effectively unless we can identify and overcome those biases. You learnt how to do that. You learnt that in facing reality, then you can deal with it in a way that fosters growth.

The next law involved flexibility. As Epictetus put it, you can only use what is in your power. You have to roll with the punches. Flexibility helps you to make whatever changes you need to make when you are faced with an unexpected challenge. It allows you to think of ways to adjust your approach toward your goal while maintaining the goal.

We touched on the inevitability of suffering and pain, and why you need to accept that as part of your cup, and how you can quiet your mind despite it all. No one can lead well if they are not able to master themselves. We worked up to chapter nine, where you learnt to apply reason to your emotion, whether it is anger or stress. All through, I tried to provide practical tips and techniques that you can start applying today. I tried to make the book as applicable to real life as stoic wisdom is.

You have everything you need to look at how you spend your time and what things you are doing to improve your resilience, build an unbreakable mind, and conquer your fears. You know that even though the shadow of death looms over all of us, as long as it has not claimed us, we get to make a good and impactful life by first bringing our minds to order. So now the question is whether you will do it. Will you embody the laws in this book? I hope your answer is yes.

THANK YOU!

Thank you so much for buying my book.

I know you had many options to pick from but you picked this one.

Because of that, I am grateful. Thank you for reading it to the end. I hope that you have gotten what you came here for and then some.

Before you go, I need to ask for a small favor from you. **Would you kindly post a review of the book? Leaving a review is the easiest and best way to support our work.**

And you know what? Your feedback helps me to keep writing books like this one that will hold

your hand toward the kind of personal changes you want to make in your life. It would mean the world to me to hear from you.

ALSO BY ALEXANDER CLARKE

Visit my author page

author.to/alexanderclarke

STOP OVER THINKING

The 34 Best Techniques to Reducing Stress,
Controlling Your Mind, Overcoming Negative
Thoughts and Living a Worry-Free Life

ALEXANDER CLARKE

REFERENCES

10 reasons why we don't stick to things. (2017, December 13). zen habits. https://zenhabits.net/wiggleroom/

33 selected stoic quotes on life and happiness (Stoicism). (2022, July 8). The Happiness Blog. https://happyproject.in/stoic-quotes-life/

Building resilience one step at a time. (n.d.). Thrive. https://thriveglobal.com/stories/building-resilience-one-step-at-a-time/

Canfield, J. (2021, November 10). *A complete guide to using the law of attraction.* Jack Canfield. https://jackcanfield.com/blog/using-the-law-of-attraction/

REFERENCES

Clear, J. (2020, February 3). *The scientific argument for mastering one thing at a time.* James Clear. https://jamesclear.com/master-one-thing

Ferry. (2018, October 15). Forbes. https://www.forbes.com/sites/forbescoachescouncil/2019/08/27/a-quiet-mind-is-a-high-performance-mind/?sh=19a1ab3e66eb

Four ways social support makes you more resilient. (n.d.). Greater Good. https://greatergood.berkeley.edu/article/item/four_ways_social_support_makes_you_more_resilient

Holl, K. (2021, July 13). *Find your focus: Stick to the ONE thing ~ Kristi Holl.* Kristi Holl. https://www.kristiholl.com/find-your-focus-stick-to-the-one-thing/

Hone. (2019, September 25). *The three secrets of resilient people.* YouTube. https://www.youtube.com/watch?v=NWH8N-BvhAw

How to endure and overcome the worst of life's hardships. (2013, March 5). Lifehack. https://www.lifehack.org/articles/communication/how-to-endure-and-overcome-the-worst-of-lifes-hardships.html

How to face & overcome challenges in life with confidence. (2021, February 23). Chopra. https://chopra.com/articles/how-to-face-overcome-challenges-in-life-with-confidence

How to focus on the good things in life (When times are tough). (2021, February 18). Lifehack. https://www.lifehack.org/900282/focus-on-the-good

Keller, G., & Papasan, J. (2013). *The ONE thing: The surprisingly simple truth behind extraordinary results.* Bard Press.

Lagacé, M. (2022, February 21). *100 stoic quotes for a wiser perspective on life – WisdomQuotes.* Wisdom Quotes. https://wisdomquotes.com/stoic-quotes/

Leading by putting people first: What does that mean & how do you do it? (2020, July 21). LinkedIn. https://www.linkedin.com/pulse/leading-putting-people-first-what-does-mean-how-do-you-jacob-morgan

Lollydaskal. (2019, November 13). *The best ways leaders quiet mind chatter - Lolly Daskal | Leadership.* Lolly Daskal. https://www.lollydaskal.com/leadership/the-best-ways-leaders-quiet-mind-chatter/

Radford, & Trogden. (2020). Forbes. https://www.forbes.com/sites/civicnation/2022/06/28/better-together-partnering-student-affairs-and-academic-affairs-in-advancing-nonpartisan-college-student-voter-engagement-efforts/?sh=5624d1a375ae

Stoicism?, W. I. (2022, April 20). *How to think like a stoic, learn like a stoic, live like a stoic.* Medium. https://medium.com/stoicism-philosophy-as-a-way-of-life/how-to-think-like-a-stoic-learn-like-a-stoic-live-like-a-stoic-11ecff67b534

Truong, D. M. (n.d.). *Focus on the good things in life.* Moral Stories. https://moralstories.top/read/focus-on-the-good-things-in-life

What makes some people more resilient than others (Published 2020). (2020, June 21). The New York Times - Breaking News, US News, World News and Videos. https://www.nytimes.com/2020/06/18/health/resilience-relationships-trauma.html

Why some people are more resilient than others. (2015, March 11). Psychology Today. https://www.psychologytoday.com/us/blog/good-thinking/201503/why-some-people-are-more-resilient-others

Wiebe, J. (2022, May 13). *5 ways to strengthen your support system*. Talkspace. https://www.talkspace.com/blog/how-to-strengthen-your-support-system/

Made in the USA
Las Vegas, NV
15 August 2023

76152560R00269